LABOUR WELFARE & LABOUR LEGISLATION – 2

(SYLLABUS AND STUDY MATERIAL)

PROJECT MSW,

DEPARTMENT OF SOCIAL WORK,

PSG COLLEGE OF ARTS AND SCIENCE, COIMBATORE,

COPRIGHT BELONGS TO ALL STUDENT OF SOCIAL WORK DEPARTMENT

(2012 – 2014 BATCH)

CREATOR: T.M.SURESH

CONTENT CREATOR: G.SANTHOSH

CONTRIBUTERS: THIVYA VILASHINI

AND ALL MSW STUDENTS

I0426136

SYLLABUS

UNIT I:

Labor and labour welfare – concept of labour – concept of labour welfare – important constituent functions of implementing and enforcing authority under various legislations – principle of labour welfare – theories of labour welfare.

UNIT II:

Social security and ILO – concept of social security – meaning, objectives, need for social security responsibility of state to producing social security need based through insurance scheme constrains extending social assistance significance and condition of social insurance – importance and conditions – public provident fund – importance, recommendation of NCL 1969 – International Labour Organisation.

Functions – conventions and recommendation – impact of ILO in India.

UNIT III:

Wage and bonus – concept of wage – meaning – minimum wage – living wage – need base fair wage – factors of wage fixation – concept of wage board – meaning – need – objectives, functions – national wage policy – payment of wages act 1936 – minimum wages act 1948 – the equal remuneration act 1976 – the concept of bonus – meaning – payment of bonus act 1965.

UNIT IV:

Industrial housing and workers education – concept of industrial housing – importance – housing condition of industrial cities in India – problem of housing – effect, remedial measures – difference housing schemes – role of HUDCO – Tamilnadu housing board – Tamilnadu clearance board – 3 tire system of housing scheme – promotion of housing colonies – concept of workers education – meaning, scope, need, objectives, schemes of workers education – role of central board for education – role of productivity council – social security legislation.

UNIT V:

Employee state insurance act

Employee's provident fund and miscellaneous profusions act.

Provident fund/ public provident fund.

Employees deposit linked insurance scheme 1976

Employees pension scheme1995.

Payment of gratuity act 1972 – TN payment of subsistence act 1981 – TN conferment of permanent status act 1981 – workmen's compensation act 1923.

STUDY MATERIALS

UNIT I:

Labor and labour welfare – concept of labour – concept of labour welfare – important constituent functions of implementing and enforcing authority under various legislations – principle of labour welfare – theories of labour welfare.

Labor:

1. Labor is a person who sells his service for a profit (pay/wage)
2. Physical presence is felt
3. Better welfare is called labor welfare
4. Anything done for betterment of labor is called labor welfare(Physical   betterment,   mental   betterment, environment betterment)

ᵕ Classification

- Intramural (inside org)
- Extramural (outside org)
- Social assistance (govt.)/ social welfare (by govt./inst/employer)
- Labor welfare is dynamic concept which is changing and ever changing
- Labor welfare committee started on1969 it is created condition ofwell Being, happiness, satisfaction, conservation and betterment of HR.
- It is a social concept as it community society and state implies well being of individuals in turn.
- Labor welfare is the adoption of measures to promote physical, social, psychological, and general being of working population
- By providing labor welfare facilities it gives sense of belongingness to the week place.
- It will raise the normal living of the employees to a standard of living.
- It contributes to more efficiency of the employee resulting in productivity.

LABOUR WELFARE

Labour welfare activities in an industrialized society has far reaching impact not only on the work force but also all the facets of human resources. Labour welfare includes all such activities, which not only secures existential necessities but also ensures improvement in spiritual and emotional quotient. It comprises of short term and long terms goal toward building a humane society.

As labour welfare is a dynamic concept, changes in its principles activities and the rationale supporting them have not been static. They closely follow the stages of advancement of the industrialized society – from police Theory to Functional Theory. Accordingly principles for successful implementation of labour welfare activities ranges from adequacy of wages to impact on efficiency as well as transformation of personality in nut shell, it is extension of democratic values in an industrialized society.

Theories of Labour welfare Activities have been formulated on the conviction that it is man behind the machine who is responsible for achieving mission of an organization. A person can deliver at his best only when he is satisfied and committed to the cause. To keep the employees motivated and committed various welfare facilities are provided by the organization not only to the employees but also to their family member too.

The term 'Welfare' expresses many ideas, meanings and connotations, such as the state of well being, health, happiness, prosperity and the development of human resources. It includes both the social and economic aspects of welfare. The social concept of welfare implies the welfare of man, his family and his community. All these three aspects are inter-related and work together. The economic aspect of welfare covers promotion of economic development by increasing production and productivity.

Welfare is also called a relative concept, for it is related to time and space. Changes in it have an impact on the system of welfare as well. As welfare is growing and dynamic, the welfare potential changes, as a result of which its content keeps on varying and has to keep pace with the changing times. Also the characteristics of welfare vary for it depends of a nation in all fields. Its meaning and components, therefore, differ from country to country and from place to place.

The economic welfare activities are such, which can be brought directly or indirectly into relation with money, Pigou[1] defined economic welfare as that part of social welfare that can be brought directly or indirectly into relation with the measuring need of money. According to him, "the economic welfare of a community of a given size is likely to be greater, the larger is the share that accrues to the poor." However, he admitted that economic welfare was not the index of total welfare.

The word labour means any productive activity. In a broader sense, therefore the phrase labour welfare means the adoption of measures to promote the physical, social, psychological and general well being of the working population. Welfare work in any industry aims or should aim at improving the working and living conditions of workers and their families.

The concept of labour welfare activities, however, is flexible, elastic and differs from time to time, region to region, industry to industry and country to country, depending upon the value system, level of education, social customs, degree of industrializations and the general standard of the socio-economic development of a people.

It is also related to the political situation in a country. Further it depends upon the kinds of problems with which society is confronted as well as on the structure of the industry. It is molded according to the age group, sex, socio-cultural background, marital status, economic status and educational level of the employees in various industries.

DEFINITION OF LABOUR WELFARE
Labour welfare has been defined in various ways, though no single definition has found universal acceptance. The Oxford dictionary defines labour welfare as "Efforts to make life worth living for workmen." Chambers dictionary defines welfare as "A state of faring or doing well. Freedom from calamity, enjoyment of health and prosperity[2]".

The Encyclopedia of Social Science defines it as "the voluntary efforts of the employers to establish, within the existing industrial system, working and sometimes living and cultural conditions of employees beyond what is required by law, the customs of the industry and the condition of market"[3].

In the Report II of the ILO Asian Regional conference, it has been stated that worker's welfare may be understood to mean "such services, facilities and amenities, which may be established outside or in the vicinity of undertakings, to enable the persons employed therein to perform their work in healthy and congenial surroundings and to provide them with the amenities conducive to good health and high morale." [4]

The Labour Investigation committee (1944-46) includes under labour welfare activities "anything done for the intellectual, physical, moral and economic betterment of the workers, whether by employers, by government or by other agencies, over and above what is laid down by law or what is normally expected as per of the contractual benefits for which the workers may have bargained." [5]

The Report of the Committee on Labour welfare (1969) includes under it "such services, facilities and amenities as adequate canteens, rest and recreation facilities, sanitary and medical facilities, arrangements for travel to and from work and for the accommodation of workers employed at a distance from their homes and such other services, amenities and facilities including social security measures as contribute to improve the conditions under which worker are employer." [6]

Thus, the whole field of welfare is said to be one "in which much can be done to combat the sense of frustration of the industrial workers, to relieve them of personal and family worries, to improve their health, to afford them means of self expression, to offer them some sphere in which they can excel others and to help them to a wider conception of life". [7] It promotes the well-being of workers in variety of ways.

LABOUR AND LABOUR WELFARE

Labour sector addresses multi-dimensional socio-economic aspects affecting labour welfare, productivity, living standards of labour force and social security. To raise living standards of the work force and achieve higher productivity, skill upgradation through suitable training is of utmost importance. Manpower development to provide adequate labour force of appropriate skills and quality to different sectors is essential for rapid socioeconomic development. Employment generation in all the productive sectors is one of them basic objectives. In this context, efforts are being made for providing the environment for self-employment both in urban and rural areas. During the Ninth Plan period, elimination of undesirable practices such as child labour, bonded labour, and aspects such as ensuring workers' safety and social security, looking after labour welfare and providing of the necessary support measures for sorting out problems relating to employment of both men and women workers in different sectors has received priority attention.

EVOLUATION OF LABOUR WELFARE CONCEPTS

The term Labour Welfare lends itself to different interpretations and had always the same significance in different countries.

To have a look over the evaluation of labour welfare concepts, different definitions and thoughts related to labour welfare need to be considered. The transition from home production to the modern factory system took place in Europe and America from about 1750 to 1830, a period coinciding with the Industrial Revolution in England.

Although mankind as a whole benefited greatly by the Industrial Revolution, misunderstanding began to undermine the sympathy and cooperation that had previously existed between the employer and the employees. Discontent and fiction began to exist at home and shop as a result of misunderstanding and more gap develop between the employers and their workers. The workers in a single group previously numbered a handful began to number hundreds and thousands. Previously, the employers enjoyed the friendship of their associates at the bench, gradually became impossible. He could know them only causally, by faces and names, perhaps not their weakness and their strength, their interests, their ambitions, their hobbies etc. They became to him merely a group of workers whose labour must be bought. Without the employer's knowledge and probably against their real purposes, they came into being an attitude on the part of management towards the workers that has become known as the 'Commodity Concept of Labour".

Over the passage of time other concepts are developed:

Most common concepts of labour welfare are described below:

1.   Commodity Concept:

Wages were higher when the supply of labour as scarce in relation to the demand for labour and wages were low, when supply was substantially in excess of the demand for it. This gave rise to the idea that labour, affected by the law of supply and demand, was like a commodity, the price of which was determined by the supply and the demand for it.

2.   Machinery Concept:

The commodity conception overlooked the fact that the employer bought and sold, not the actual labour, but the products the labour produced. He determined the value of labour by the value of the goods and profit. The employers thus started to regard their employees largely as operating organisms or machine capable of a certain amount of out-put. Just as we try to purchase machinery and plant with the lowest direct outlay, so we can hire labour as cheaply as possible. Just as we try to keep plant and equipment operating economically as long as possible and junk them for better when necessary, so we can use and discard human labour.

3.   Charity Concept:

According to this, the human sufferings were the manifestations of divine justice for the sin committed by the sufferers. It was the duty of those who were in fortunate positions to assist those who are in need. Charity was given for salvation of the donar or out of human sentiments and with pity towards the distrssed.

Thus labour welfare was mainly based on human and religious motive and social workers were conceived as kind hearted persons who devoted their efforts to the care and protection of the needy and the distressed people of the society.

4.   Paternalistic Concept:

It is a concept that management started to assume a fatherly and protective attitude towards employees, partially to suppress the movement of union.

It is not believed that merely supplying many benefits such as housing, recreation and pensions make a management paternalistic. It is the attitude and the manner of installation that determine whether or not a management is peternal in its dealings with employees. To be paternalistic, two characteristics are necessary.

Firstly, the profit motive should not be prominent in management's decision to provide such employees services. They should be offered because the management has decided that the employee needs them, just as a parent decides what is good for his children.

Secondly, the decision concerning what services to provide and how to provide them belongs solely to management. The father makes the decision that the feels is the best for the child.

5.   Natural Resource Concept:

Some statesmen began to conceive of labour as natural resources, which the state should protect. Out of this conception came child labour laws, restrictions of hours of women workers, workmen's compensation and Health ans Safety Legislation.

6.   Democratic Concept:

It is also know as citizenship concept. The workers are considered as citizens of the industry in which they are employed and entitled to a right to have a voice in terminating the rules and regulations under which they work. The result of this realization was industrial democracy with its shop committee, industrial councils, employee representation plans and so on.

7   Partnership Concept:

The partnership relationships imply mutual responsibilities as well as the sharing of the fruits of the joint endeavours. The earliest efforts to translate this idea in to action were the fostering of stock-ownership plans. Recently, profit sharing has come into prominence. Some argue that the partnership concept is fallaciousthat their can be no mutuality of interest between owner who are seeking large profits and workers who desire high wages that the two interests are incompatible and cannot be reconciled.

8.   Social Welfare Concept:

In the past, social welfare was mainly based on humanitarian and religious motives. This concept, in course of time, became inadequate and unsatisfactory to meet the needs of modern societies.

The modern concept of social welfare is based on the recognition of the rights and worth of the individuals. It is characterized by an "organized effort through a range of programme, services and agencies to promote social well-being and to prevent or alleviate social malfunctioning". In short, social welfare is conceived with a broad range of activities and programmes directed to human well-being.

The profession of social work accepts the following main principles:

Social work accepts the importance and dignity of every man and rejects the jungle doctrine of the survival of the fittest.

It recognizes that human sufferings are undesirable and should be prevented or at least alleviated whenever possible.

All classes of persons in the community have an equal right to the social services; there is community responsibility to provide services; without discrimination to all.

The adoption of this conception towards labour is becoming increasingly widespread. In short, citizenship, partnership and social welfare conceptions are at present playing very important roles in industrial welfare activities.

Important Constitution Policy For Labour Law

CHAPTER-III (Articles-16,19,23&24)
- Human labour
- Need for protecting
- Safe guarding

CHAPTER-IV (Articles-39,41,42,43,43A&54)
- Fundamental Rights
- Directive principles of state policy
- Union List
- Entry No.55: Regulation of labour and safety in mines and oil fields.
- Entry No.61: Industrial disputes concerning union employees
- Entry No.65: Union agencies and institutions for
- " Vocational......... training............"
- Concurrent List
- Entry No.22 : Trade unions Industrial and labour disputes
- Entry No.23 : Social Security and insurance, employment and unemployment
- Entry No.24 : Welfare of about including conditions of work, provident funds, employers invalidity and old age pension and maternity benefit
- Legislation can be categorized

Labour law enacted by Central Government
- Enforced both by Central and State Government
- Enacted- CG
- Enforced – SG

- Enacted,Enforced - RS

Directive principles
- For Securing the health and strength of employees, men and women
- For Securing the health and strength of employees, men and women
- That the tender age of children are not abused
- That citizens are not forced by economic necessity to enter avocation unsuited to their age or Strength
- Just and human condition of work and maternity relief and provide
- That the government shall take steps, by suitable legislation or in any other way to secure the participation of employee in the management of undertakings establishment or other organization engaged in any industry

EXTRA NOTES

LABOUR LEGISLATION.

Industrialisation creates a number of social and economic problems like employment of women and children, minimum wages, trade unions, insanitary living quarters and deplorable working conditions in the factories, etc. Labour laws are, therefore, enacted to facilitate their solutions, as ordinary civil laws are inadequate to meet them. The State has adopted a progressive policy, and is keeping pace with the labour policy of the Government of India and the standard laid down by the International Labour Organisation. This has produced a plethora of legislation and their administration. These laws also deal with the regulation of industrial relations between the management and the workers.

The salient features of the Central and State Labour Acts in force in the district are given hereunder : The Indian Factories Act of 1948 provides for the health, safety and welfare of the workers. The Punjab Shops and Commercial Establishment Act, 1958, regulates the conditions of work and terms of employment of workers engaged in shops, commercial establishments, theatres, restaurants, etc. The Punjab Maternity Benefit Act, 1943, provides for the grant of cash benefits to women workers for specified periods before and after confinements. The Employment of Children Act, 1938, prohibits the employment of young children below the age of 15 years in certain risky and unhealthy occupations. The payment of wages Act, 1936, regulates the k\timely payment of wages without any unauthorized deductions by the employers. The Minimum Wages Act, 1948, ensures the fixation and revision of minimum rates of wages in respect of certain scheduled industries involving hard labour. The Industrial Disputes Act, 1947, provides for the investigation, and settlement of industrial disputes by mediation, conciliation, adjudication and arbitration., there is scope for payment of compensation in cases of

lay-off and retrenchment. The Industrial Employment (Standing Orders) Act, 1946, requires employers in Industrial establishments to define precisely the conditions of employment under them and make them known to their workmen. These rules, once certified, are binging on the parties for a minimum period of six months. The Workmen's Compensation Act, 1923, provides for compensation to injured workmen of certain categories and in the case of fatal accidents to their dependants if the accidents arose out of and in the course of their employment. It also provides for payment of compensation in the case of certain occupational diseases. The Indian Trade Unions Act, 1926, recognizes the right of workers to organise into trade unions, when registered, have certain rights and obligations and function as autonomous bodies. The Employees' State Insurance Act, 1948, provides for sickness benefit, maternity benefit, disablement benefit and medical benefit. The Employees' Provident Fund Act, 1952, seeks to make a provision for the future of industrial worker after he retires or in case he is retrenched, or for his dependents in case of his early death. The Punjab Industrial Housing Act, 1956, provides for the administration allotment, realization of rent, etc., in connection with quarters constructed under the Subsidized Industrial housing Scheme
.

The labour welfare work, thus, covers a wide range of activities and in its present form is widely recognised and is regarded as an integral part of the industrial system and management.

The labour laws in the State are administered by the Labour Department headed by the Labour Commissioner, Punjab. The Employees' State Insurance Act, 1948, and the Employees' Provident Fund Act, 1952, are however, operated under the direction of the Employees' State Insurance Corporation and the Regional Provident Fund Commissioner, Punjab, respectively. The Labour Commissioner is assisted in his work by the Chief Inspector of Factories at the State headquarters, Labour Officers at circle level, and Factory Inspectors and Labour Inspectors and other staff at district below :

THE WORKING OF IMPORTANT LEGISLATIVE ENACTMENTS IS GIVEN BELOW :

Industrial Relations. – The relations between the employees and the employer are governed by the Industrial Disputes Act, 1947, and the machinery provided under it is two-fold one is for the prevention of disputes by providing internal machinery in the form of Works Committee and Welfare Officers, and the other consists of a permanent Conciliation Officer, Conciliation Board, Court of Inquiry and Industrial Tribunal./ the Conciliation Officer, Ludhiana, is responsible for enforcing the provisions of the Act. He fosters good relations between the two sides of industry by removing, as far as possible, the causes of friction and by timely redress of grievances of the parties.

Even though the functions of the Conciliation Officer are purely advisory and he has no direct power to make or vary awards or agreements, he has been successful in bringing about a large number of agreements between the parties.5

There has been no major strike in Ludhiana District during 1965 and 1966, except a general strike by the textile workers of Ludhiana in the months of March-April, 1965, which lasted for ten days.

WORKS COMMITEES

Under the Industrial Disputes Act, 1947, the factories or industrial establishments employing more than 100 persons are required to constitute a works committee for securing and preserving amity and good relations between the employers and the workmen. A works committee consists of representatives of employers and workmen engaged in the establishment, so that the number of representatives of workmen in the committee shall not be less than the number of representatives of the employers. Accordingly, 26 factories in the district come under the purview of this clause.

Trade Unions.- Trade unions are voluntary organisation of workers formed to promote and protect their interests by collective action. As the trade unions are the most suitable organisations for adjusting relations between the employers and the employees, they have acquired an important place in the economic, political and social life of the community.

Ever since the attainment of Independence, trade union movement in the district has gained considerable momentum and there has been a constant increase in the number of registered trade unions. The particulars of the trade unions, registered under the Indian Trade Union Act, 1926,
 which functioned in the district at the end of 1966, are given in Appendix at pages 610-12.

The Indian Factories Act, 1948. – All the Factories Acts from 1934 to 1947 were repealed and a new Act called the Factories Act, 1948, was enacted. It incorporates several provisions for the welfare of labour. To enforce the provisions of the Act and to look after the general welfare of the employees, Labour Welfare Officers have been provided in three factories at Ludhiana.

Employees' Provident Fund Scheme. – The wages of industrial workers are not so high as to enable them to accumulate substantial savings. When old age or illness renders them unfit for earning, they are forced to lead a life of object poverty and misery.

The joint-family system in its traditional form, has outlived its utility and to save the old and destitute workers from starvation deaths, there must be provisions like that of provident fund. In the event of worker's pre-mature deaths, their dependants are left without any means of subsistence. The Employees' Provident Fund Scheme, framed by the Government of India under the employees' Provident Fund Act, 1952, and enforce on November 1, 1952, attempts to remedy this unhappy situation.

In Ludhiana District, by December 31, 1966, 424 factories/establishments with an employment strength of 12,089 workers were covered by the

Act. Of these, about 7,932 workers contributed to the scheme.

Provision has also been made under the Act to grant advances to the members for payment of premiums on their life insurance policies, for purchase of dwelling sites or houses, for construction of a house, for meeting the expenses in case of serious illness, etc.

To afford timely financial assistance to the nominees/ heirs of the deceased members, a Death Relief Fund was set up in 1964. A minimum of Rs. 500 is assured by way of relief. A non-refundable advance is also granted in case of the individuals' retrenchment in order to mitigate the immediate hardship caused by such an eventuality.

Employees' State Insurance Scheme. – Sickness is another important risk to be guarded against. The question of instituting a health insurance scheme had been engaing the attention of the Government of India from 1927 onwards and ultimately led to the passing of the Employees' State Insurance Act in 1948.

The scheme is compulsory wherever applicable and all workers covered under the Act must be insured. The Act, however, does not apply to a member of the armed forces or to a person whose remuneration in the aggregate exceeds Rs. 500 a month.

The Act makes provisions for the following benefits to insured person, or, as the case may be, to their dependants : sickness benefit, maternity benefit, disablement benefit, dependants' benefit, and medical benefit. The benefits under the first four categories are in cash, while medical benefit is in kind. The employees' State Insurance Amendment Act, 1966, introduced "Funeral Benefit" under which an amount not exceeding Rs. 100 is paid to the claimants towards expenditure on the funeral of the deceased insured persons.

The Employees' State Insurance Scheme was inaugurated by the late Prime Minister, Shri Jawaharlal Nehru, on February 24, 1952, at Kanpur (Uttar Pradesh). It was extended to 7 towns in the Punjab,

including Ludhiana, on May 17, 1953. The schemewas implemented at Khanna from February 27,1966.

The 7 cities and towns in the then Punjab State, to which the Employees' State Insurance Scheme was extended on May 17, 1953, were : Amritsar, Ambala, Jullundur, Batla, Abdullapur, Bhiwani and Ludhiana. since then, the scheme has been extended to other areas also.

A local office of the Employees' State Insurance is functioning at Ludhiana with three pay-offices at Khanna, Abohar (Ferozepore District) and Kharar (Ropar District).7 At Ludhiana, the medical facilities are provided to the insured persons through Panel System. A dispensary is functioning at each of the three attached centres.

By March 31, 1966, there were 17,750 insured persons at Ludhiana besides 700 at one of the attached stations at Khanna. During 1965-66, there were 320 factories covered under the scheme at Ludhiana and Khanna in respect of which 260 accident reports were received in the local office at Ludhiana in respect of Ludhiana and Khanna. The total amount of cash benefit paid to the insured persons during the same year in respect of these two stations was Rs. 1,13,910.92.

Subsidised Industrial Housing Scheme. - Housing is unquestionably one of the vital problems for the industrial workers since housing and health are inter-connected and both affect industrial efficiency. The Government of India have, therefore, been making sustained efforts to encourage and assist the industrialists to build houses for their workers. The scheme formulated in 1946 and 1949 for this purpose did not prove satisfactory. It was, therefore, decided to offer more liberal terms of financial assistance to the State government, employers and workers for the construction of residential houses. Accordingly, in pursuance of the recommendations in the First Five-Year Plan, in September, 1952, the Subsidised Industrial Housing Scheme was introduced. Certain important modifications were made in the Scheme in 1953.

Under the Subsidised Housing Scheme, there are three types of tenements for the purpose of subsidies and loans : those put up by the State Governments or Statutory bodies, such as Improvement Trusts ; those put up by the industrial employers for the use of labourers in their employ : and those put up by co-operative housing societies of workers. The State Government, thus, constructed colonies in Ludhiana for the industrial workers in the Industrial Area 'B'. Each colony consisted of 126 one-room houses and 124 two-room houses, to be allotted to industrial workers at a nominal rent of Rs 10 and Rs 16, per mensem, respectively.

Labour Welfare Centre. – Started in 1953, a Labour Welfare Centre is working at Ludhiana under the Labour Commissioner, Punjab, Chandigarh. It provides educational as well as recreational facilities to industrial workers and their children. The women are imparted training in tailoring and embroidery. In-door and out-door games are organised in the centre for the workers and a radio-set and musical instruments are provided for recreation. There is a library for the use of workers. Cultural and variety programmes are also organised occasionally in the centre for the entertainment of the workers.

PRINCIPLES:-
PRINCIPLES FOR SUCCESSFUL IMPLEMENTATION OF WELFARE ACTIVITIES
The success of welfare activities depends on the approach which has been taken into account in providing such activities to the employees. Welfare policy should be guided by idealistic morale and human value. Every effort should be made to give workers/ employees some voice in the choice of welfare activities so long as it does not amount to dictation from workers.

There are employers who consider all labour welfare activities as distasteful legal liability. There are workers who look upon welfare activities in terms of their inherent right. Both parties have to accept welfare as activities of mutual concern. Constructive and lasting Progress in the matter of social justice can be achieved only if welfare activities are accepted as essential factors in the progress of the business organization

Labour welfare is dependent on certain basic principles. The following are the principles on which successful implementation of welfare programmes depends :

- Principles ofadequacy of wages
- Principles of social responsibility in India
- Principles of efficiency
- Principles of repersonalisation
- Principles oftotality of welfare
- Principles of co-ordination and integration
- Principles of democratic values and association
- Principles of responsibility
- Principles of accountability
- Principles of timelines
- Principles of self help.

Adequacy of Wages:
Labour welfare measures cannot be a substitute for wages. Workers have a right to adequate wages. But high wage rates alone cannot create healthy atmosphere, nor bring about a sense of commitment on the part of workers. A combination of social welfare, emotional welfare and economic welfare together would achieve good results.

Social Liability of Industry:
Industry, according to this principle, has an obligation or duty towards its employees to look after their welfare. The constitution of India also emphasizes this aspect of labour welfare.

Impact on Efficiency:
This plays an important role in welfare services, and is based on the relationship between welfare and efficiency, though it is difficult to measure this relationship. Programmes for housing, education and training, the provision of balanced diet and family planning measures are some of the important programmes of labour welfare which increases the efficiency of the workers, especially in underdeveloped or developing countries.

Increase in Personality:
The development of the human personality is given here as the goal of industrial welfare which, according to this principle, should counteract the baneful effects of the industrial system. Therefore, it is necessary to implement labour welfare services. Both inside and outside the factory, that is, provide intra-mural and extra-mural labour welfare services.

Totality of Welfare:
This emphasizes that the concept of labour welfare must spread throughout the hierarchy of an organization. Employees at all levels must

accept this total concept of labour welfare programme will never really get off the ground.

Co-ordination or Integration:
This plays an important role in the success of welfare services. From this angle, a co-ordinated approach will promote a healthy development of the worker in his work, home and community. This is essential for the sake of harmony and continuity in labour welfare services.

Democratic Values:
The co-operation of the worker is the basis of this principle. Consultation with, and the agreement of workers in, the formulation and implementation of labour welfare services are very necessary for their success. This principle is based on the assumption that the worker is "a mature and rational individual." Industrial democracy is the driving force here. Workers also develop a sense of pride when they are made to feel that labour welfare programmes are created by them and for them.

Responsibility:
This recognizes the fact that both employers and workers are responsible for labour welfare. Trade unions, too, are involved in these programmes in healthy manner, for basically labour welfare belongs to the domain of trade union activity. Further, when responsibility is shared by different groups, labour welfare work becomes simpler and easier.

Accountability:
This may also be called the Principle of Evaluation. Here, one responsible person gives an assessment or evaluation of existing welfare services on a periodical basis to a higher authority. This is very necessary, for then one can judge and analyze the success of labour welfare programmes.

Timely:
The timeliness of any service helps in its success. To identify the labour problem and to discover what kind of help is necessary to solve it and when to provide this help are all very necessary in planning labour welfare programmes. Timely action in the proper direction is essential in any kind of social work.

Last, but not the least is the fact that labour welfare must aim at helping workers to help themselves in the long run. This helps them to become more responsible and more efficient there are some theories which constitutes the conceptual frame framework of the labour welfare, describe these theories Several theories constituting the conceptual framework of labour welfare have so far been outlined these are

- Policy theory
- Religious theory
- Philanthropic theory
- Trusteeship theory
- Placating theory
- Public relations theory
- Functional theory

THE CONCEPT OF LABOUR WELFARE ESTABLISHED ON SEVEN THEORIES. THEY ARE:

- The Police Theory
- The Religious Theory
- The Philanthropic Theory
- The Trusteeship Theory or Paternalistic Theory
- The Placating Theory
- The Public Relations Theory
- The Functional Theory.

Policy theory:

This theory is based on the contention that a minimum standard of welfare is necessary for workers. The assumption on which the theory is based is the without compulsion, supervision and fear of punishment, no employer will provide even the barest minimum of welfare facilities for workers this theory is based on the assumption that man is selfish and self –centered, and always tries to achieve his own ends, even at the cost of the welfare of others. According to this theory, owners and managers of industrial undertakings make use of every opportunity to engage in this kind of exploitation. The sate has therefore to step in to prevent exploitation by enacting stiff laws to coerce industrialists into offering a minimum standard of welfare to their workers. Such interference it is felt is in the interests of the progress and welfare of the state as well. Laws are enacted to compel management to provide minimum wages, congenial working conditions and reasonable hours of work and social security.

The policy theory involves several stages of implementation

- Enactments
- Periodical supervision
- Punishment

Religious theory

The theory views were an essentially religious. Religious feelings are what sometimes prompt employers to take up welfare activities in the belief of benefits either in his life or in support after life. Any good work is considered an investment, because both the benefactor and the beneficiary are benefited by the good work done by the benefactor. This theory does not take into consideration that the workers are not beneficiaries but rightful claimants to a part of the gains derived by their labour.

Philanthropic theory

Philanthropy is the inclination to do or practice of doing well to ones fellow men. Man is basically self centered and acts of these kinds stem from personal motivation, when some employers take compassion on their fellowmen, they may undertake labor welfare measures for their workers.

Trusteeship theory

In this theory it is held that the industrialists or employers holds the total industrial estate, properties and profits accruing form them in trust for the workmen, for himself , and for society. It assumes that the workmen are like minors and are not able to look after their own interests that they are ignorant because of lack of education. Employers therefore have the moral responsibility to look after the interests of their wards, who are the workers.

Placating theory

As labour groups are becoming better organized and are becoming demanding and militant, being more conscious of their rights and privileges that even before, their demand for higher wages and better standards increases. The placing theory advocates timely and periodical acts of labour welfare to appease the workers.

Public relations theory

This underlining philosophy behind this theory is an atmosphere of goodwill between management and labour and also between management and the public. Labour welfare programms under this theory, work as assort of an advertisement for companies and helps build up good and healthy public relations. The labour welfare movements may be utilized to improve relations between management and labour. An advertisement or an exhibition of alobour welfare programme may help the management projects a good image of the company.

FUNCTIONAL THEORY OF LW:

`This theory is otherwise called efficiency theory, here welfare is used as a means to secure, preserve, and develop the efficiency of the labor and the productivity of organization. By providing welfare measures the benefit is enjoyed by both the management and labor. Not only the welfare measures even the labor actively participate in the management decision making and help the labor to improve efficiency, it is possible only when a good and healthy relationship prevail between trade union of the management.

- Labor laws enforced and enhanced by central govt.
- Labor laws enacted by central govt. and enforced by both central and state govt.
- Labor laws enacted by central govt. and enforced by state govt.
- Labor laws enacted and enforced by state govt.

ENFORCED AND ENACTED BY CG:

- Emp. State Insurance Scheme, 1948.
- Emp. Provident fund and Misc. act, 1952
- The Dock Workers (health, safety, welfare) act, 1986.
- Mines act, 1952.

- Mica Mines Labor (welfare fund) act, 1946.
- The Beedi Workers (welfare) act, 1976.
- The Cine workers (welfare) act, 1981.
- The Beedi workers Welfare Fund act, 1976.
- The Cine Workers Welfare Fund act, 1981.
- The Iron ore mines, magnesium, ore mines and chromium ore mines Labor Welfare act, 1976.
- The Iron ore mines, magnesium, ore mines and chromium ore mines Labor Welfare Fund act.
- Limestone and Dolomite Mines Welfare Fund act, 1972

ENACTED BY CG AND ENFORCED BY BOTH CG AND SG:

- The Child Labor(prohibition and abolition) act, 1986.
- The Building and other construction workers (regulation of employment and conditions of service) act, 1996.
- Industrial Dispute act, 1947.
- Industrial Employment (standing orders) act, 1946.
- Equal Remuneration act, 1976.
- Inter-state Migrant Workman (regulation of employment and conditions of service) act, 1979.
- Labor Laws act, 1988.
- Maternity Benefit act, 1961.
- Minimum Wages act, 1948.
- Payment of Bonus act, 1965.
- Payment of Gratuity act, 1972
- Payment of Wages act, 1936.
- Apprenticeof act, 1961
- Contract Labor (regulation of abolition) act, 1970.
- Cine Workers and Cinema Theater Workers (Regulation of employment) act, 1981.

ENACTED BY CG AND ENFORCED BY SG:

- Factories act 1948
- Motor transport workers act 1968
- Personal injuries (compensation and insurance) act 1963
- Personal injuries (emergency provision) act 1962
- Plantation act 1951
- Sales promotion employees (condition of service) act 1976
- Trade union act 1926
- The weakly holidays act 1942
- The working journalist and other newspaper employees(condition of service and misc. provision) act 1955
- Workmen compensation act 1923
- Employment exchange(compulsory notification of vacancy) act 1959
- Bonded labor system(abolition) act 1976

- Beedi and cigar workers act(conditions of employment) 1976

II. ENACTED BY SG AND ENFORCED BY SG:
- Tamilnadu shops and establishment act 1947
- Tamilnadu catering establishment act 1958
- Tamilnadu handloom workers act 1981
- Tamilnadu manual workers act 1982
- Tamilnadu industrial establishment act 1988

UNIT II:
Social security and ILO – concept of social security – meaning, objectives, need for social security responsibility of state to producing social security need based through insurance scheme constrains extending social assistance significance and condition of social insurance – importance and conditions – public provident fund – importance, recommendation of NCL 1969 – International Labour Organisation.
Functions – conventions and recommendation – impact of ILO in India.

SOCIAL SECURITY
Social security is the protection that a society provides to individuals and households to ensure access to health care and to guarantee income security, particularly in cases of old age, unemployment, sickness, invalidity, work injury, maternity or loss of a breadwinner.

Social security protection is clearly defined in ILO conventions and UN instruments as a basic human right – albeit one that a small proportion of the people on our planet actually enjoy. Broadly defined as a system of contribution- based health, pension and unemployment protection, along withtax-financed social benefits, social security has become a universal challenge in a globalizing world.
Only 20 percent of the world's population has adequate social security coverage, while more than half lacks any kind of social security protection at all. Those without coverage tend to be part of the informal economy – they are generally not protected in old age by social security, and they cannot afford to pay their health care bill. In addition, many people have insufficient coverage – that is, they may lack significant elements of protection (such as health care or pension) or what protection they do have is low or declining. Experience shows that people are willing to contribute to social security benefits that satisfy their priority needs.

It was once assumed that an increasing proportion of the labour force in developing countries would end up in formal-sector employment covered by social security. However, experience has shown that the growing incidence of informal work has led to stagnant or declining rates of coverage. Even in countries with high economic growth, increasing numbers of workers – often women – are in less secure employment, such as casual labour, home work and certain types of self-employment

THE ILO AND SOCIAL SECURITY

Social security was established as a basic human right in the ILO's Declaration of Philadelphia (1944) and its Income Security Recommendation, 1944 (No. 67). This right is upheld in the Universal Declaration of Human Rights, 1948, and the International Covenant on Economic, Social and Cultural Rights, 1966.

ILO conventions and recommendations relevant to social security extension policies include:

• The Social Security (Minimum Standards) Convention, 1952 (No. 102)
• The Equality of Treatment (Social Security) Convention, 1962 (No. 118)
• The Employment Injury Benefits Convention, 1964 (Schedule I amended in 1980) (No.121)
• Invalidity, Old-Age and Survivors' Benefits Convention, 1967 (No. 128)
• The Medical Care and Sickness Benefits Convention, 1969 (No.130)
• The Maintenance of Social Security Rights Convention, 1982 (No. 157)
• The Employment Promotion and Protection against Unemployment Convention, 1988 (No.168)
• The Job Creation in Small and Medium- Sized Enterprises Recommendation, 1998 (No. 189)
• Maternity Protection Convention (Revised) 2000 (No. 183

Impact of Social Security

Social security has a powerful impact at all levels of society. It provides workers and their families with access to health care and with protection against loss of income, whether it is for short periods of unemployment or sickness or maternity or for a longer time due to invalidity or employment injury. It provides older people with income security in their retirement years. Children benefit from social security programmes designed to help their families cope with the cost of education. For employers and enterprises, social security helps maintain stable labour relations and a productive workforce. And social security can contribute to social cohesion and to a country's overall growth and development by bolstering living standards, cushioning the effects of structural and technological change on people and thereby providing the basis for a more positive approach toward globalization

SOCIAL SECURITY

" A programme of protection provided by the society against the contingencies of modern life – sickness, unemployment, old age, dependency, industrial accident and invalidism against which the individual cannot expected to protect himself and his family by his own ability or foresight"-

- FRIEDLANDER

CONCEPT OF LABOUR SECURITY

Social Security may broadly be defined as "the security that society furnishes through appropriate organisation, against certain risks for its members". Such risks are generally contingencies like:

- Employment injury
- Sickness
- Invalidism
- Disablement
- Industrial disease
- Maternity
- Old age
- Widowhood
- Orphanage
- Unemployment

The concept of social security varies from place to place and time to time. Social security measures have the following main characteristics :
They are established by law or practice
They provide some forms of cash payment to the individual to at least partly compensate for the loss of income.
The benefits or services are provided in there major ways viz., Social Insurance, Social Assistance and Public Services

- Objectives Of Social Security
- To increase productivity
- To improve health and control sickness
- To prevent occupational diseases
- To remove the mental and physical hazards
- To take care of old age
- Various legislation are implemented

SOCIAL INSURANCE:

Social Insurance is a mechanism through which benefits are provided to the contributories (out of contributions made by them, the employers and the government) necessary for satisfying wants during old age, sickness, unemployment and other contingencies of life.

CHARACTERISTICS:

- It is financed mainly from the common monetary contribution from employees, employers, and the state.
- Major contribution is from the state and the employer and a nominal amount from each worker according to his capacity to pay.
- Whenever there is total or partial loss of income, social insurance benefits take care of the minimum standard of living within the limits.
- Benefits are granted without an examination of individual needs and without any means tests and without affecting the sense of self-respect of the beneficiary.

- Benefits are so planned as to cover all those who need to be covered on a compulsory basis.
- Social insurance aims at reducing the suffering arising out of the contingencies faced by the individual.
- It is different from commercial insurance which is voluntary and whose benefits are proportionate to the premium paid. It also offers protection against the individual risks and does not guarantee a minimum standard of living.

Advantages:
It raises moral values and relieves physical and mental distress which afflicts a vast majority of people.

Disadvantages:
There is a feeling that it would weaken incentive to work among the beneficiaries.
A properly planned Social Insurance Scheme should have the following components:
a) Sickness and invalidity insurance.
b) Accident insurance.
c) Maternity insurance.
d) Unemployment insurance.
e) Old-age insurance.
f) Survivor insurance.

PUBLIC PROVIDENT FUND (PPF)

Meaning
Public Provident Fund (PPF) is a savings-cum-tax-saving instrument in India. It also serves as a retirement-planning tool for many of those who do not have any structured pension plan covering them. The account can be opened in designated post offices, SBI branches and branches of some nationalized banks. ICICI banks was the first private sector bank which was authorized to open PPF accounts.

Eligibility
Individuals who are residents of India are eligible to open an account under the Public Provident Fund scheme. A PPF account may be opened under the name of a minor by his/her legal guardian. However, each person is eligible for only one account under his/her name.
Non-resident Indians (NRIs) are not eligible to open an account under the Public Provident Fund Scheme. However a resident who becomes an NRI during the 15 years' tenure prescribed under Public Provident Fund Scheme, may continue to subscribe to the fund until its maturity on a non-repatriation basis.

Investment and Returns
A minimum yearly deposit of Rs. 500 is required to open and maintain a PPF account, and a maximum deposit of Rs.100000/ can be made in a PPF account in any given financial year. The investments can be made in

multiples of Rs. 500, either as a whole sum, or in installments (not exceeding 12 in a year, though more than one deposit can be made in a month). The credit to the PPF account is made on the date of clearance of the cheque, not on the date of its presentation

Every subscription should be made in cash or through a crossed cheque or draft or postal order, in favour of the accounts office, at the place at which that office is situated. In case of any cheque, draft or postal order should be drawn at a bank or post office at that place. It is also possible to transfer funds online using net banking in a PPF account opened with SBI also NEFT Transfer from any bank is possible with sbi ppf accounts.

The government of India decides the rate of interest for PPF account. The current interest rate effective from 1 April 2013 is 8.70% Per Annum(compounded annually). Interest is calculated on the lowest balance between the close of the fifth day and the last day of every month. Till March 2010, cheques deposited for clearing, up to 5th of the month were eligible for that month's interest. Since 29 March 2010, only the amounts which are actually cleared on or before the 5th of the month are eligible for that month's interest.

The minimum tenure of the PPF account is 15 years, which can be further extended in blocks of 5 years each for any number of blocks. The extension can be with or without contribution. An account holder, continuing with fresh subscription, can withdraw up to 60% of the balance to his credit at the commencement of each extended period in one or more installments but only once in a year.

Nomination facility is available. In the case of joint nominees, it is possible to allocate the percentage of benefits to each nominee.

Features

The public provident fund is established by the central government. One can voluntarily open an account with any nationalized bank or post office. The account can be opened in the name of individuals including minor.

The minimum amount is Rs.500 which can The rate of interest at present is 8.7% per annum, which is also tax-free. The entire balance can be withdrawn on maturity. Interest received is tax free.

The maximum amount which can be deposited every year is Rs. 1,00,000 in an account. The interest earned on the PPF subscription is compounded. All the balance that accumulates over time is exempt from wealth tax. Moreover, it has low risk – risk attached is Government risk. PPF is available at post offices and banks.

Disadvantages of PPF

The problem with PPF is its lack of liquidity. One can withdraw the investment made in 1st year only in 7th year. However, loan against investment is available from 3rd financial year. If liquidity is not an issue, you should invest as much as you can in this scheme before looking for other fixed income investment options.

Second problem is debasement of currency and governments inflation policy as PPF unlike physical assets will not cover a person for inflation, especially in the current economic scenario in 2013. Inflation has been substantially above the PPF interest rate for well over 5 years; as PPF Interest rate of 8.8 or 8.7% as at April 2013 is far below the double digit cpi inflation rate of 11% and way below the real inflation rate.

The worst of PPF
1. The interest rate keeps changing
2. Lengthy lock-in period
3. Interest is calculated on the lowest balance
4. Lack of liquidity

NATIONAL LABOR COMMISSION & INDUSTRIAL RELATIONS POLICY OF 1969
Recognition of Unions and role of IRC:
- 100 or more workers in establishment - compulsory
- At least 30% of the workers within the organization
- 25% if recognition is sought for industry in a local area.
- The IRC must certify the union as a representative union by
- Examination of membership records or
- Holding an election by secret ballot open to all employees.
- The other aspects : the level of recognition to be offered, certifying the majority union, and dealing with other related matters.
- The rights- Right to sole representation,
- Right to enter into collective agreements
- The right to collect membership subscriptions
- The right of check-off, etc.

Minority unions must only be allotted the right to represent cases of dismissal and discharge of their members before the Labor Court.
Unions must be made strong, organizationally, and financially. Nevertheless, intra-union disputes must be discouraged.

Strikes/Lock-outs and Gheraos:
1. If cessation of work may cause social harm, strikes should be banned; instead, the case must be forwarded to an arbitration committee.
2. Every strike must be preceded by a warning.
3. A maximum of one month must be allotted for holding a legal strike.
4. Gherao is not really a form of labor unrest because it involves physical compulsion instead of economic pressure.
5. Penalties should be charged for unjustified strikes
6. Compensation and wages should be distributed to prevent unnecessary strikes.
7. Conciliation:
8. Conciliation is most effective if it is uninfluenced by external factors, and the conciliation department is adequately staffed.
9. Arbitration:

10.   Voluntary arbitration will be accepted
11.   Unfair Labor Practices:
12.   Penalties should be levied upon those who participate in unfair labor practices

ILO

Structure & Working

The ILO accomplishes its work through three main bodies, all of which comprise government, employer and worker representatives. International Labour Conference Meet at the International Labour Conference in June of each year, in Geneva

Two government delegates, an employer delegate and a worker delegate. Technical advisors assist the delegations, which are usually headed by Cabinet Ministers who take the floor on behalf of their governments.

The Conference establishes and adopts international labour standards , Organization's budget and elects the Governing Body.

The Governing Body E xecutive council of the ILO meets three times a year in Geneva. takes decisions on ILO policy and establishes the programme and the budget, which it then submits to the Conference for adoption. also elects the Director-General. composed of 28 government members, 14 employer members and 14 worker members.

States of chief industrial importance permanently hold ten of the government seats.
Government representatives are elected at the Conference every three years, taking into account geographical distribution.

The employers and workers elect their own representatives respectively. The International Labour Office Permanent secretariat of the I L O

It is the focal point for ILO's overall activities, which it prepares under the scrutiny of the Governing Body and under the leadership of a Director-General, who is elected for a five-year renewable term
.
The Office employs some 1,900 officials of over 110 nationalities at the Geneva headquarters and in 40 field offices around the world. In addition, some 600 experts undertake missions in all regions of the world under the programme of technical cooperation. The Office also contains a research and documentation centre and a printing facility, which issue many specialized studies, reports and periodicals.

Tripartism : The ILO aims to ensure that it serves the needs of working women and men by bringing together governments, employers and workers to set labour standards, develop policies and devise programmes. Its tripartite structure makes the ILO unique among world organizations because employers' and workers' organizations have an equal voice with governments in all its deliberations.

Technical Cooperation : ILO's technical cooperation and capacity-building programmes help to build bridges between the ILO's standard-setting role and the people. An extensive network of offices throughout Africa, Asia, Latin America, Central and Eastern Europe and the Middle East provides technical guidance on policy issues, and assistance in the design and implementation of development programmes.

Labour law reform   Labour administration and dispute settlement Strengthening the ability of employers' and workers' organizations to engage in organizing and bargaining collectively

- Awareness raising
- Finance of ILO
- ILC fixes budget on recommendations of the Governing Body
- Member States make contributions
- Contributions fixed on ad-hoc basis from year to year
- India's contribution : 2.77% (7th)
- Impact of ILO on India
- 2 Fold impact

Ratified ILO standards : Principal source of Labour Legislation after incorporation into existing Labour Laws

Effect of Art. 3 : nomination of non-govt delegates & advisors to ILC (furthering process of organization among employers and workers in India)
Conventions & Recommendations

Conventions : are international treaties and are instruments, which create legally binding obligations on the countries that ratify them.

Recommendations : are non-binding and set out guidelines orienting national policies and actions.
The government reports are examined by the Committee of Experts on the Application of Conventions and Recommendations, composed of some twenty independent, eminent figures in either the legal or social field and who are also specialists in labour matters. The Committee submits an annual report to the International Labour Conference, which is closely examined by a tripartite committee composed of government, employer and worker members

Legal Framework on wages, working conditions, welfare, social security etc in India have been significantly influenced by the ILO C & Rs

The ILO's Governing Body has identified eight conventions as "fundamental", covering subjects that are considered as fundamental principles and rights at work

Approach of India with regard to International Labour Standards has always been positive. India had ratified 39 of the 184 conventions. It has ratified 4 of the 8 core conventions of ILO

- Fundamental conventions
- Freedom of Association and Protection of the Right to Organise Convention, 1948 (No. 87)
- Right to Organise and Collective Bargaining Convention, 1949 (No. 98)
- Forced Labour Convention, 1930 (No. 29)*
- Abolition of Forced Labour Convention, 1957 (No. 105)*
- Minimum Age Convention, 1973 (No. 138)
- Worst Forms of Child Labour Convention, 1999 (No. 182)
- Equal Remuneration Convention, 1951 (No. 100)*
- Discrimination (Employment and Occupation) Convention, 1958 (No. 111)*
- Governance conventions
- Labour Inspection Convention, 1947 (No. 81)
- Employment Policy Convention, 1964 (No. 122)
- Labour Inspection (Agriculture) Convention, 1969 (No. 129)
- Tripartite Consultation (International Labour Standards) Convention, 1976 (No. 144)

Active partnership policy & multi-disciplinary team

Child Labor Legislations
In India, within a framework of the Child Labor (Prohibition and Regulations) Act, 1986 and through the National Policy on Child Labor, ILO has funded the preparation of certain local and industry specific projects. In two projects, viz. Child Labor Action and Support Programmes (CLASP) and International Programme on Elimination of Child Labor (IPEC), the ILO is playing a vital role

IMPACT OF ILO IN INDIA.
India is a founder member of the International Labour Organization, which came into existence in 1919. At present the ILO has 175 Members. A unique feature of the ILO is its tripartite character. The membership of the ILO ensures the growth of tripartite system in the Member countries. At every level in the Organization, Governments are associated with the two other social partners, namely the workers and employers. All the three groups are represented on almost all the deliberative organs of the ILO and share responsibility in conducting its work. The three organs of the ILO are:
International Labour Conferences: - General Assembly of the ILO – Meets every year in the month of June.

Governing Body: - Executive Council of the ILO. Meets three times in a year in the months of March, June and November.

International Labour Office: - A permanent secretariat.

The work of the Conference and the Governing Body is supplemented by Regional Conferences, Regional Advisory Committees, Industrial and Analogous Committees, Committee of Experts, Panels of Consultants, Special Conference and meetings, etc.

INTERNATIONAL LABOUR CONFERENCE

Except for the interruption caused by the Second World War, the international Labour Conference has continued, since its first session in 1919 to meet at least once a year. The Conference, assisted by the Governing Body, adopts biennial programme and budget, adopts International Labour Standards in the form of Conventions and Recommendations and provides a forum for discussing social economic and labour related issues. India has regularly and actively participated in the Conference through its tripartite delegations.

The Conference has so far had 4 Indian Presidents viz., Sir. Atul Chatterjee (1927), Shri Jagjivan Ram, Minister for Labour (1950), Dr. Nagendra Singh, President, International Court of Justice (1970) and Shri Ravindra Verma, Minister of Labour and Parliamentary Affairs (1979). There have also been 8 Indian Vice Presidents of the International Labour Conference, 2 from the Government group, 3 from the Employers and 3 from the Workers' Group. Indians have chaired the important Committees of the Conferences like Committee on Application of Standards, Selection Committee and Resolutions Committee.

GOVERNING BODY

The Governing Body of the ILO is the executive wing of the Organization. It is also tripartite in character. Since 1922 Indian has been holding a non-elective seat on the Governing Body as one of the 10 countries of chief industrial importance. Indian employers and workers' representatives have been elected as Members of the Governing Body from time to time.

Four Indians have so far been elected Chairman of the Governing Body. They are Sir Atul Chatterjee (1932-33), Shri Shamal Dharee Lall, Secretary, Ministry of Labour (1948-49), Shri S.T. Merani, Joint Secretary, Ministry of Labour (1961-62) and Shri B.G. Deshmukh, Secretary, Ministry of Labour (1984-85).

The Governing Body of ILO functions through its various Committees. India is a member of all six committees of the Governing Body viz. (i) Programme, Planning & Administrative; (ii) Freedom of Association; (iii) Legal Issues and International Labour Standards; (iv) Employment & Social Policy; (v) Technical Cooperation and (vi) Sectoral and Technical Meetings and Related issues.

THE INTERNATIONAL LABOUR OFFICE

The International Labour Office, Geneva provides the Secretariat for all Conferences and other meetings and is responsible for the day-to-day implementation of decisions taken by the Conference, Governing Body etc. Indians have held positions of importance in the International

Labour Office. Special mention must be made of Shri S.K. Jain who retired as Deputy Director General of the ILO. Shri Gopinath is currently the Director International Institute of Labour Studies, Geneva.

INTERNATIONAL LABOUR STANDARDS - ILO CONVENTIONS: -

The principal means of action in the ILO is the setting up the International Labour Standards in the form of Conventions and Recommendations. Conventions are international treaties and are instruments, which create legally binding obligations on the countries that ratify them. Recommendations are non-binding and set out guidelines orienting national policies and actions

.

Pakistan (34), Japan (45), Australia (57), China (20), Malaysia (14), Sri Lanka (39) and USA (14).

The approach of India with regard to International Labour Standards has always been positive. The ILO instruments have provided guidelines and useful framework for the evolution of legislative and administrative measures for the protection and advancement of the interest of labour.

To that extent the influence of ILO Conventions as a standard for reference for labour legislation and practices in India, rather than as a legally binding norm, has been significant. Ratification of a Convention imposes legally binding obligations on the country concerned and, therefore, India has been careful in ratifying Conventions. It has always been the practice in India that we ratify a Convention when we are fully satisfied that our laws and practices are in conformity with the relevant ILO Convention. It is now considered that a better course of action is to proceed with progressive implementation of the standards, leave the formal ratification for consideration at a later stage when it becomes practicable. We have so far ratified 39 Conventions of the ILO, which is much better than the position obtaining in many other countries. Even where for special reasons, India may not be in a position to ratify a Convention, India has generally voted in favour of the Conventions reserving its position as far as its future ratification is concerned.

Core Conventions of the ILO: - The eight Core Conventions of the ILO (also called fundamental/human rights conventions) are:

- Forced Labour Convention (No. 29)
- Abolition of Forced Labour Convention (No.105)
- Equal Remuneration Convention (No.100)
- Discrimination (Employment Occupation) Convention (No.111)
- (The above four have been ratified by India).
- Freedom of Association and Protection of Right to Organised Convention (No.87)
- Right to Organise and Collective Bargaining Convention (No.98)
- Minimum Age Convention (No.138)

Worst forms of Child Labour Convention (No.182)

(These four are yet to be ratified by India)

Consequent to the World Summit for Social Development in 1995, the above-mentioned Conventions (Sl.No. 1 to 7) were categorised as the Fundamental Human Rights Conventions or Core Conventions by the ILO. Later on, Convention No.182 (Sl.No.8) was added to the list.

As per the Declaration on Fundamental Principles and Rights at Work and its Follow-up, each member State of the ILO is expected to give effect to the principles contained in the Core Conventions of the ILO, irrespective of whether or not the Core Conventions have been ratified by them.

Under the reporting procedure of the ILO, detailed reports are due from the member States that have ratified the priority Conventions and the Core Conventions every two years. Under the Follow-up to the ILO Declaration on Fundamental Principles and Rights at Work, a report is to be made by each member State every year on those Core Conventions that it has not yet ratified.

REASONS FOR NON-RATIFICATION:
CONVENTIONS NO.87 AND 98:

Convention No.87 provides for the right of workers and employers, without any distinction to establish and join organizations of their own choosing without previous authorisation. Their organizations have the right to form or join federations and confederations, including on the international level. These organizations or federations may not be liable to arbitrary dissolution or suspension by an administrative authority. The only exception provided for in the Convention to the right to organise "without distinction whatsoever" are the armed forces and the police, to whom special rules and regulations may apply. Convention No.98 aims to protect the exercise of the right to organise and to promote voluntary collective bargaining. The guarantees provided for under these two Conventions are by and large available to workers in India by means of constitutional provisions, laws and regulations and practices. The main reason for our not ratifying these two Conventions is the inability of the Government to promote unionisation of the Government servants in a highly politicised trade union system of the country. Freedom of expression, freedom of association and functional democracy are guaranteed by our Constitution. The Government has promoted and implemented the principles and rights envisaged under these two Conventions in India and the workers are exercising these rights in a free and fare democratic society. Our Constitution guarantees job security, social security and fair working conditions and fair wages to the Government servants. They have also been provided with alternative grievance redressal mechanisms like Joint Consultative Machinery, Central Administrative Tribunal etc. Hence, our stand has been that this section of the workforce cannot be said to have been deprived of the right of association.

CONVENTION NO.138

As of now, there is no omnibus provision in our labour laws prohibiting children below certain age from doing any work whatsoever. For ratifying Convention No.138, enactment of a suitable all encompassing Central

Legislation for minimum age of entry to employment would need to be enacted to have provisions for:

(a)   fixing a minimum age of 14 years for admission to employment or work in all occupations, employment and work but excluding agriculture in family and small holdings producing for own consumptions and not regularly employing hired workers; and

(b)   fixing a minimum age of not less than 18 years for admission to any type of employment or work which by its nature or circumstances in which it is carried out is likely to jeopardise the health, safety or morals of young persons.

The definition of 'child' in all concerned existing legislations would then need to be determined in accordance with the provisions of the Central Legislation on minimum age for admission to employment. Thus, the Bill on the above lines on its enactment was to replace or supercede the concerned existing legislations like the Child Labour (Prohibition and Regulation) Act, 1986 etc.

Fixing of minimum age for admission to employment needs to be preceded by creation of suitable enforcement machinery and measures as would warrant the children not being compelled by circumstances to seek employment. The setting up of such machinery, particularly, for the unorganised sector in agriculture, cottage and small-scale industries etc., (except for those industries which are covered under the Factories Act) becomes a difficult task in a developing country like India.

In the background of the above position, consultations have been held with the concerned Ministries/Departments and State Governments to examine the existing provisions of national laws and practices on the subject vis-à-vis the provisions of the Convention. Since there is no omnibus law on minimum age for entry into employment and the existing laws prescribe different minimum ages for different sectors, the process is likely to be long drawn.

CONVENTION NO.182:
Ratification of Convention No.182 concerning Worst Forms of Child Labour is being pursued by the ILO with all member countries. The ILO has also initiated a concerted campaign for this purpose. India is examining the feasibility of ratifying this convention in consultation with the concerned Central Ministries and State Governments. This is also to be discussed in a tripartite forum with the participation of the Employers and Workers Representatives.

Action taken so far:
 Consultation meeting taken by Secretary (Labour) on 3rd July, 2001 with the representatives of Central Ministries/Departments and selected State Governments: In this meeting it was felt that there would not be any

objection to agreeing to the elimination of worst forms of child labour is defined in Article 3(a), (b) and (c). In this connection, the concerned Ministries have been approached and they have also agreed to amend the existing Acts in such a manner as to bring them in line with the definitions in Convention No.182. It was felt that Article 3(d) of the Convention was more omnibus and less definitive in its nature. The work defined under this clause would need to be decided through the tripartite mechanisms as defined in Article 4 of the Convention.

Tripartite meeting of the Tripartite Committee on Conventions on 19th October, 2001: The meeting decided that the provisions of Article 3(a), (b)&(c) of Convention No.182 were acceptable as given in the text. As far as the provision of Article 3(d) was concerned, wherein the Tripartite consultation mechanism was required to identify hazardous occupations and processes, the Technical Advisory Committee constituted under the Child Labour (Prohibition and Abolition) Act would be requested to examine the list of hazardous activities and identify the occupations and processes that were likely to harm the health, safety and morals of children as defined in Article 3(d) of Convention No.182. The matter would then be placed before the next tripartite meeting, by which time the report of the Second National Labour Commission was also expected to be available. The views of the social partners on the list of hazardous occupations identified by the Technical Advisory Committee would also be elicited before the next meeting is convened.

ILO AREA OFFICE, NEW DELHI
An ILO Branch Office was set up in New Delhi in 1929. The work of the Branch Office consisted of collecting and disseminating information and maintaining links with the Government of India and the Organizations of Employers and Workers and generally to publicise the work of ILO among the Indian audience. With the planned programme of decentralisation, the Branch Office became an Area Office of ILO in 1970. The Area Office at New Delhi has been changing in its jurisdiction over the years. It now coordinates technical assistance activities in diverse focus as such as rural Labour, women workers, employment generation, occupational safety and health, population control, family welfare, etc. in India and Bhutan.

ILO COMMITTEE OF EXPERTS
Prominent Indians have served on the ILO Committee of Experts on Application of Conventions and Recommendations, which is an independent body to oversee the implementation of the ILO Conventions by Member countries. The Members of the Committee of Experts are appointed in their individual capacity from among persons of independent, standing and are drawn from all parts of the world. Indian who have been members of the Committee include:

Justice P.N. Bhagwati, Retd. Chief Justice of India - Since 1978.
Justice P.V. Gajendragadkar - 1972-1977
Shri A. Ramaswamy Mudaliar - 1959-1970
Shri R.M. Bannerjee - 1956-1988
Shri Atul Chatterjee - 1936-1938 & 1945-1955.

ACTIVE PARTNERSHIP POLICY & MULTI-DISCIPLINARY TEAM
One of the major reforms initiated recently is the launching of the "Active Partnership Policy" whose aim is to bring ILO closer to its constituents. The main instrument for implementation of the policy – is the multi-disciplinary team, which will help identify special areas of concern and provide technical advisory services to member States to translate ILO's core mandate into action. The multi-disciplinary team for South-Asia is based in New Delhi. It consists of specialists on employment, industrial relations, workers and employers' activity, small-scale enterprises and International Labour Standards.

ILO AND CHILD LABOUR
ILO's interest in child labour, young persons and their problems is well known. It has adopted a number of Conventions and Recommendations in this regard. In India, within a framework of the Child Labour (Prohibition and Regulations) Act, 1986 and through the National Policy on Child Labour, ILO has funded the preparation of certain local and industry specific projects. In two kanor projects, viz. Child Labour Action and Support Programmes (CLASP) and International Programme on Elimination of Child Labour (IPEC), the ILO is playing a vital role.

The implementation of IPEC programmes in India has certainly created a very positive impact towards understanding the problem of child labour and in highlighting the need to elimination child labour as expeditiously as possible. A major contribution of the IPEC programme in India is that it has generated a critical consciousness among all the 3 social partners for taking corrective measures to eliminate child labour.

DECENT WORK
The concept of Decent Work is being propagated by the ILO. It encompasses four strategic objectives –

I.   Promotion of Rights at Work - It calls for renewed attention to ILO's standards, as well as a fresh look at complimentary means and instruments for achieving this goal.

II.   Employment - Creation of greater employment and income opportunities for women and men as a means to reduce poverty and inequality.

III.   Social Protection – This section emphasises expansion of social security schemes

IV.   Social Dialogue – This emphasises examining ways of strengthening the institutional capacity of ILO constituents as well as their contribution to the process of dialogue.

The concept of Decent Work emphasises that the quantity of employment should not be divorced from quality of work and stresses that a social and economic system should be evolved to ensure basic security and employment without compromising workers' rights and social standards in a highly competitive world.

Although India agrees that the four strategic objectives are necessary for decent work, this has no meaning unless we can provide an opportunity to work. Therefore, employment generation should be the focus of the all ILO programmes and activities. The basic requirement of Decent Work should be to first ensure work to any potential worker and then all other elements of the decent work concept will automatically follow. This stand of India was appreciated by other nations as well. India also made it clear in the meetings of the ILO that the concept of decent work has to be fixed keeping in mind the conditions of work in the social, economic and cultural context of each country. It cannot be made applicable uniformly to every country.

Linkage between trade and labour standards:
The issue of linkage between trade and labour standards was first raised at the conclusions of the Uruguay Round at Marrakesh in 1994 by the USA. India and other developing countries had taken the position that labour standards at the international levels can be appropriately addressed only in the ILO, not in the WTO. The social clause is not within the mandate of the WTO. In response, India had countered that the relationship between trade and immigration policies may also be examined in the WTO. The issue was not pursued seriously by the US for sometime thereafter.
The issue again came up at the First Ministerial Conference of the WTO in Singapore in 1996. In this Conference, developing countries including India once again rejected the proposal of the US to include labour standards as an agenda in the WTO. The final Ministerial Declaration at Singapore endorsed the stand of the developing countries and reiterated the following:

    i.   ILO is the competent body to set and deal with core labour standards and WTO affirms its support in promoting such standards.

    ii.   It rejected the use of labour standards for protectionist purposes and agreed that the comparative advantage of countries, particularly low wage developing countries, must in no way be put into question.

iii. It noted that the WTO and ILO Secretariats would continue their existing collaboration.
The Ministerial Declaration at Singapore was seen by the developing countries as a successful heading off of further moves towards linkage between trade and labour standards and confining discussions within the

ILO.

In the Third WTO Ministerial Conference held at Seattle in 1999, the US had proposed establishment of a Working Group on Trade and Labour, which would deal with issues such as trade and employment, trade and social protection, core labour standards, forced and child labour, etc. and submits a report for consideration at the Fourth Ministerial Conference. The European Union proposed the establishment of a joint ILO-WTO Working Forum on trade, globalisation and labour issues to promote better understanding of the issues involved through a substantial dialogue between all interested parties including governments, employers, trade unions and other international organizations. There was no conclusive outcome from this Conference, which attracted much criticism and demonstrations by NGOs and other activist groups.

The Fourth Ministerial Conference of the WTO, which was held in Doha from 9th to 14th November 2001, reaffirmed the Declaration made at the Singapore Ministerial Conference of the WTO that ILO is the appropriate forum to set and deal with the issues of core labour standards.

India's future stands on linkages issue
India will continue to adhere to the stand that all matters related to international labour standards are to be agitated only in the relevant forum of the ILO and that the comparative advantage of countries, particularly developing countries, must in no way be put into question. India will continue to reject the use of labour standards for protectionist purposes and any attempt to link labour standards with trade will be vehemently opposed invariably, even if isolated by other countries.

UNIT III:
Wage and bonus – concept of wage – meaning – minimum wage – living wage – need base fair wage – factors of wage fixation – concept of wage board – meaning – need – objectives, functions – national wage policy – payment of wages act 1936 – minimum wages act 1948 – the equal remuneration act 1976 – the concept of bonus – meaning – payment of bonus act 1965.

WAGE AND BONUS – CONCEPT OF WAGE – MEANING – MINIMUM WAGE – LIVING WAGE – NEED BASE FAIR WAGE – FACTORS OF WAGE FIXATION ALL ARE EXPALAINED UNDER PAYMENT OF WAGES ACT 1936 – MINIMUM WAGES ACT 1948 – THE EQUAL REMUNERATION ACT 1976 WAGE BOARD

WHAT IS A WAGE BOARD
Wage board is a triplicate body, having representation of employers and labour besides, independent members. The representatives of the former two interests are nominated by their central organizations; others are nominated by the government. It is an important machinery of state regulation of wages.

GROWTH AND DEVELOPMENT OF WAGE BOARD

- Industrial dispute act was enacted under which wage regarding disputes could be settled through adjudication.
- The parties were not satisfied with that, thus the idea of setting up a triplicate wage board was mooted and endorsed in first plan.
- The second plan determine wages through industrial wage boards.
- It consists of equal representative of employers and workers and an independent chairman for a acceptable decision.
- First wage board was set up in cotton textiles and sugar industries.

COMPOSITION OF WAGE BOARD

- It is a tripartite representing the interests of labour, management and the public.
- Labour and management representatives are maintained in equal numbers by the government.
- These board are chaired by government nominated members representing the public

FUNCTIONS OF WAGE BOARD

- Recommending the minimum wage.
- Differential cost of living compensation.
- Regional wage differentials.
- Gratuity.
- Hours of work, etc.
- They have to
- Determine the category of workers to be brought under wage fixation.
- Work out the wage structure based on principles of fair wages.
- Workout the principles of bonus.

EVALUATION OF WAGE BOARDS

- Majority boards are of the recommendations of wage unanimous.
- They take more time to complete their task.
- Implementing the decisions are difficult.

WAGE POLICY

Wage Policy are principles acting as guidelines for determining a wage structure.

Initially as an economic issue it was mainly the concern of the employer while state was adopting laissez faire policy. But, with the industrial progress and subsequent industrial balance between employers, employees, wage bargain has become a matter for three fold concern of the employer, employee, and the state

In India it is built around certain cardinal principles:

- Equal pay for equal work
- Living wages for all workers so that they lead a decent life
- Payment of wages on appointed dates without unauthorized deductions
- Resolving wage related issues through collective bargaining
- Payment of statutory bonus at 8.33 percent as per legal provisions
- Ensuring a fair, equitable wage plan for various employees without significant wage differences.
- The capacity to pay(according to supreme court ruling- 'an employer who cannot pay minimum wages has no right to exist'

Determining fair wages over and above minimum wages with due regards to (i) the productivity of labour (ii) the prevailing level of wages (iii) the level of national income and distribution (iv) the place of industry in the economy of the company.

- To compensate for the rise in cost of living
- Economic Objectives of Wage Policy:
- Full employment and optimum allocation of all resources
- The highest degree of economic stability consistent with an optimum rate of economic progress
- Maximum income security for all sections of the community
- Social Objectives of Wage Policy:
- The elimination of exceptionally low wages
- The establishment of 'fair' labour standards
- The protection of wage earners from the effects of rising prices
- The incentive for workers to improve their productive performance

Wage Policy is a democratic set up so it cannot be enforced by the Govt alone. Its implementation has to be secured through employers and employees organizations at bargaining table i.e. by consensus

Limitations of Wage Policy:

- Socio-economic setup of our society
- Enforcement in unorganized sector
- Lack of unity among unions
- Prices rise almost beyond Govt's regulatory capabilities
- Wages lag far behind labour productivity
- Lesser number of workers in organized sector take away bulk of wages than unorganized
- Wage incomes are consumption oriented rather than savings oriented so increased wages would mean increased consumption. Therefore economic growth may not be

affected positively as it depends upon rate of investment possible through savings.
- Ever increasing addition to workforce yet dearth of skilled labour
- High wages may force employer to shift towards capital intensive methods
- High wages reduce capital for growth

Wage Policy in India
First Five Year Plan (1951-56) suggested:
- Pre-war levels of real wages be restored as a first step towards 'living wages' through increased productivity
- Reduction of disparities in income
- Reduction of gap between existing and living wages
- Standardization and maintenance of wage differentials to provide incentives

Second Five Year Plan (1956-61) stressed:
- Improvement in wages through increased productivity
- Improved layout of plants, working conditions
- Application of system of payment by result
- Improvement in management practices
- Recommended settlement of industry wise wage disputes through tripartite wage boards

Third Five Year Plan (1961-66) reinforced:
- Wage policy of preceding two plans
- Rationalization of work load/ work methods and functions of management

Three Annual plans (1966-69) aims at framing Wage Policy after taking considering:
- Price level
- Employment level
- Social Justice
- Capital required by firm for future growth

Fourth Five Year Plan (1969-74) emphasized:
- Price stability
- Extension of system of payment by results

Fifth Five Year Plan (1974-79) recommended:
- That the reward system in terms of wages and
- non-wage benefits must be related to performance records
- A wage structure to narrow down disparities within the organized sector itself.

- Govt. to intervene in setting up of wages & prices

Sixth Five Year Plan (1980-85) stressed on:
- The need for bringing about a greater rationalization of wage structure and linking of wages at least in some measure to labour productivity.
- Modernization in industry
- Evolve wage structure without restrictions on negotiations

Seventh Five Year Plan (1985-90) asserted that:
- There is a need for improvement in capacity utilization, efficiency and productivity
- Rise in levels of real income
- Reduction in disparities
- Sectoral shifts in desired directions

Eighth Five Year Plan (1992-97) focused on:
- Formulation of wage policy relating to child labour, bonded labour, rural labour, women labour and inter-state migrant labour.

THE PAYMENT OF WAGES ACT, 1936
Application of the Act:
The Act will apply to persons employed in any factory or employed (otherwise than in a factory) upon any railway by a railway administration or, either directly or through a sub-contractor, by a person fulfilling a contract with a railway administration, and to persons employed in an industrial or other establishment.

Here "factory" means a factory as defined in section 2(m) of the Factories Act, 1948 (63 of 1948) and includes any place to which the provisions of that Act have been applied under section 85(1) thereof.
"Industrial or other establishment" means any-

(a)Tramway service, or motor transport service engaged in carrying passengers or goods or both by road for hire or reward;

(b)Air transport service other than such service belonging to, or exclusively employed in the military, naval or air forces of the Union or the Civil Aviation Department of the Government of India;
(c)Dock, Wharf or Jetty;

(d)Inland vessel, mechanically propelled;

(e)Mine, Quarry or Oil-field;

(f)Plantation;

(g)Workshop or other establishment in which articles are produced, adapted or manufactured, with a view to their use, transport or sale;

(h)Establishment in which any work relating to the construction, development or maintenance of buildings, roads, bridges or canals, or relating to operations connected with navigation, irrigation, or to the supply of water or relating to the generation, transmission and distribution of electricity or any other form of power is being carried on.

2.This Act applies to wages payable to an employed person in respect of a wage period if such wages for that wage period do not exceed Rs 6500/- per month or such other higher sum which, on the basis of figures of the Consumer Expenditure Survey published by the National Sample Survey Organisation, the Central Government may, after every five years, by notification in the Official Gazette, specify.".

Meaning of wages
"Wages" means all remuneration (whether by way of salary, allowances, or otherwise) expressed in terms of money or capable of being so expressed which would, if the terms of employment, express or implied, were fulfilled, be payable to a person employed in respect of his employment or of work done in such employment, and includes-
(a)Any remuneration payable under any award or settlement between the parties or order of a court;
(b)Any remuneration to which the person employed is entitled in respect of overtime work or holidays or any leave period;
(c)Any additional remuneration payable under the terms of employment (whether called a bonus or by any other name);
(d)Any sum which by reason of the termination of employment of the person employed is payable under any law, contract or instrument which provides for the payment of such sum, whether with or without deductions, but does not provide for the time within which the payment is to be made;
(e)Any sum to which the person employed is entitled under any scheme framed under any law for the time being in force,

But does not include-

(1)any bonus (whether under a scheme of profit sharing or otherwise) which does not form part of the remuneration payable under the terms of employment or which is not payable under any award or settlement between the parties or order of a court;
(2)the value of any house-accommodation, or of the supply of light, water, medical attendance or other amenity or of any service excluded from the computation of wages by a general or special order of the State Government;
(3)Any contribution paid by the employer to any pension or provident fund, and the interest which may have accrued thereon;
(4)Any traveling allowance or the value of any traveling concession;

(5)Any sum paid to the employed person to defray special expenses entailed on him by the nature of his employment; or

(6)Any sum as gratuity payable on the termination of employment in cases other than those specified in sub-clause (d).]

Responsibility for Payment of wages

Every employer shall be responsible for the payment of all wages required to be paid under this Act
to persons employed by him and in case of persons employed,-

(a)In factories, if a person has been named as the manager of the factory under clause (f) of sub- section

(1) of section 7 of the Factories Act, 1948 (63 of 1948);

(b)In industrial or other establishments, if there is a person responsible to the employer for the supervision and control of the industrial or other establishments;

(c)Upon railways (other than in factories), if the employer is the railway administration and the railway administration has nominated a person in this behalf for the local area concerned;

(d)In the case of contractor, a person designated by such contractor who is directly under his charge; and

(e)In any other case, a person designated by the employer as a person responsible for complying with the provisions of the Act, the person so named, the person responsible to the employer, the person so nominated or the person so designated, as the case may be,
shall be responsible for such payment.

It shall be the responsibility of the employer to make payment of all wages required to be made under this Act in case the contractor or the person designated by the employer fails to make such payment.

Wage period for payment of wages

The person responsible for payment of wages shall decide the wage period. But the period shall not exceed one month.

The wages of every person employed upon or in any railway, factory or industrial or other establishment upon or in which less than 1000 persons are employed, shall be paid before the expiry of the 7th day after the last day of the wage-period in respect of which the wages are payable Any other railway, factory or industrial or other establishment that is where more than 1000 people are employed, shall be paid before the expiry of the 10th day, after the last day of thewage-period in respect of which the wages are payable.

In the case of persons employed on a dock, wharf or jetty or in a mine, the balance of wages found due on completion of the final tonnage account of the ship or wagons loaded or unloaded, as the case may be, shall be paid before the expiry of the 7th day from the day of such completion.

Where the employment of any person is terminated by or on behalf of the employer, the wages, earned by him shall be paid before the expiry of the 2nd working day from the day on which his employment is terminated.

But where the employment of any person in an establishment is terminated due to the closure of the establishment for any reason other than a weekly or other recognized holiday, the wages earned by him shall be paid before the expiry of the 2nd day from the day on which his employment is so terminated.

Deductions from Wages allowable under the Act

Deductions from the wages of an employed person shall be made only in accordance with the provisions of this Act, and may be of the following kinds only, namely:

(a)Fines: The total amount of fine which may be imposed in any one wage-period on any employed person shall not exceed an amount equal to 3% of the wages payable to him in respect of that wage-period. No fine shall be imposed on any employed person who is under the age of fifteen years. Every fine shall be deemed to have been imposed on the day of the act or omission in respect of which it was imposed. No fine imposed on any employed person shall be recovered from him by instalments or after the expiry of 90 days from the day on which it was imposed

(b)Deductions for absence from duty;

(c)Deductions for damage to or loss of goods expressly entrusted to the employed person for custody, or
for loss of money for which he is required to account, where such damage or loss is directly attributable to his neglect or default;

(d)Deductions for house-accommodation supplied by the employer or by government or any housing board set up under any law for the time being in force (whether the government or the board is the employer or not) or any other authority engaged in the business of subsidizing house-accommodation which may be specified in this behalf by the State Government by notification in the Official Gazette;

(e)Deductions for such amenities and services supplied by the employer as the State Government or any officer specified by it in this behalf may, by general or special order, authorize.
Explanation: The word "services" in 23[this clause] does not include the supply of tools and
raw materials required for the purposes of employment;

(f)Deductions for recovery of advances of whatever nature (including advances for traveling allowance or conveyance allowance), and the interest due in respect thereof, or for adjustment ofover-payments of wages. Recovery of an advance of money given before employment began shall be made from the first payment of wages in respect of a complete wage-period, but no recovery shall be made of such advances given for traveling-expenses.

(ff)deductions for recovery of loans made from any fund constituted for the welfare of labour in accordance with the rules approved by the State Government, and the interest due in respect thereof;

(fff)deductions for recovery of loans granted for house-building or other purposes approved by the State Government and the interest due in respect thereof;]

(g)Deductions of income-tax payable by the employed person;

(h)Deductions required to be made by order of a court or other authority competent to make such order;

(i)Deductions for subscriptions to, and for repayment of advances from any provident fund to which the Provident Funds Act, 1925 (19 of 1925), applies or any recognized provident fund as defined or any provident fund approved in this behalf by the State Government, during the continuance of such approval;

(j)deductions for payments to co-operative societies approved by the State Government or any officer specified by it in this behalf or to a scheme of insurance maintained by the Indian Post Office, and

(k)deductions, made with the written authorization of the person employed for payment of any premium on his life insurance policy to the Life Insurance Corporation Act of India established under the Life Insurance Corporation Act, 1956 (31 of 1956), or for the purchase of securities of the Government of India or of any State Government or for being deposited in any Post Office Savings Bank in furtherance of any savings scheme of any such government.]]

(kk)deductions, made with the written authorization of the employed person, for the payment of his contribution to any fund constituted by the employer or a trade union registered under the Trade Union Act, 1926 (16 of 1926), for the welfare of the employed persons or the members of their families, or both, and approved by the State Government or any officer specified by it in this behalf, during the continuance of such approval;

(kkk)deductions, made with the written authorization of the employed person, for payment of the fees payable by him for the membership of any trade union registered under the Trade Union Act, 1926 (16 of 1926);

(l)Deductions, for payment of insurance premium on Fidelity Guarantee Bonds;

(m)Deductions for recovery of losses sustained by a railway administration on account of acceptance by the employed person of counterfeit or base coins or mutilated or forged currency notes;

(n)Deductions for recovery of losses sustained by a railway administration on account of the failure of the employed person to invoice, to bill, to collect or to account for the appropriate charges due to that administration whether in respect of fares, freight, demurrage, wharfage and carnage or in respect of sale of food in catering establishments or in respect of sale of commodities in grain shops or otherwise;

(o)Deductions for recovery of losses sustained by a railway administration on account of any rebates or refunds incorrectly granted by the employed person where such loss is directly attributable to his neglect or default;]

(p) Deductions, made with the written authorization of the employed person, for contribution to the Prime Minister's National Relief Fund or to such other Fund as the
Central Government may, by notification in the Official Gazette, specify;]

(q) Deductions for contributions to any insurance scheme framed by the Central Government for the benefit of its employee The total amount of deductions which may be made above in any wage-period from the wages of any employed person shall not exceed-
(i)in cases where such deductions are wholly or partly made for payments to co-operativesocieties under clause (j) above, 75% of such wages, and

(ii)in any other case, 50% of such wages:
Where the total deductions authorized exceed 75% or, as the case may be, 50% of the wages, the excess may be recovered in such manner as may be prescribed.

Maintenance of registers and records
It is the responsibility of the employer to maintain such registers and records giving particulars of persons employed by him, the work performed by them, the wages paid to them, the deductions made from their wages and such other particulars. Every record and register maintained shall be preserved for a period of 3 years after the date of last entry made therein.

Rights of employees
Where contrary to the provisions of this Act any deduction has been made from the wages of an employed person, or any payment of wages has been delayed, than following persons may apply to such authority:

(1)Such person himself,
(2)Any legal practitioner or
(3)Any official of a registered trade union authorized in writing to act on his behalf, or
(4)Any Inspector under this Act, or

(5)Any other person acting with the permission of the authority appointed by the state government.

Every such application shall be presented within 12 months from the date on which the deduction from the wages was made or from the date on which the payment of the wages was due to be made, as the case may be:

Any application may be admitted after the said period of 12 months when the applicant satisfies the authority that he had sufficient cause for not making the application within such period.

When any application made is entertained, the authority shall hear the applicant and the employer or other person responsible for the payment of wages, or give them an opportunity of being heard, and, after such further enquiry, if any, as may be necessary, may, without prejudice to any other penalty to which such employer or other person is liable under this Act, direct the refund to the employed person of the amount:

(1)Deducted, or

(2)The payment of the delayed wages, together with the payment of such compensation as the authority may think fit. The amount of such compensation shall:

a)Not exceeding 10 times the amount deducted in the case where deduction has been wrongly made from the wages and;

b)Not exceeding Rs 3000/- but not less than Rs 1500/- in the case where there is delay in

payment of wages.

Even if the amount deducted or delayed wages are paid before the disposal of the application, direct the payment of such compensation, as the authority may think fit, not exceeding Rs 2000/-.

A claim under this Act shall be disposed of as far as practicable within a period of 3 months from the date of registration of the claim by the authority.

Also no direction for the payment of compensation shall be made in the case of delayed wages if the authority is satisfied that the delay was due to- (a) A bona fide error or bona fide dispute as to the amount payable to the employed person; or

(b) The occurrence of an emergency, or the existence of exceptional circumstances, the person responsible for the payment of the wages was unable, in spite of exercising reasonable diligence.

If the authority hearing an application under this section is satisfied-

(a)That the application was either malicious or vexatious, the authority may direct that a penalty not exceeding Rs 375/-to be paid to the employer or other person responsible for the payment of wages by the person presenting the application; or

(b)That in any case in which compensation is directed to be paid under the applicant ought not to have been compelled to seek redress under this section, the authority may direct that a penalty not exceeding Rs 375/- to be paid to the State Government by the employer or other person responsible for the payment of wages.

A single application can also be made by the unpaid group of the employed persons. Employed persons can be said to belong to Unpaid Group:

(1)If they are borne by the same establishment, and

a.If deductions have been made from their wages for the same wage period in contravention of the Act, or

b.Their wages for the same wage period have remained unpaid after the day fixed by the Act.

An appeal can be made against an order dismissing either wholly or part of an application made. The appeal can be made within 30 days of the date on which the order or direction was made. The appeal has to be made before the court of small causes or the District Court by following persons:

(1)By an employed person or any legal practitioner or any official of a registered trade union authorized in writing to act on his behalf or any Inspector under this Act, if the total amount of wages claimed to have been withheld from the employed person exceeds Rs 20/- or from the unpaid group to which the employed person belongs or belonged exceeds Rs 50, or

(2)By the employer or other person responsible for the payment of wages, if the total sum directed to be paid by way of wages and compensation exceeds Rs 300/- or such direction has the effect of imposing on the employer or the other person a financial liability exceeding Rs 1000/-, or

(3)By any person directed to pay a penalty.

Penalties

(1)Whoever being required under this Act to maintain any records or registers or to furnish any information or return-

(a)Fails to maintain such register or record; or

(b)Willfully refuses or without lawful excuse neglects to furnish such information or return;

or

(c)Willfully furnishes or causes to be furnished any information or return which he knows to be false; or

(d)refuses to answer or willfully gives a false answer to any question necessary for obtaining any information required to be furnished under this Act,

shall, for each such offence, be punishable with fine which shall not be less than Rs 1500/-

one but which may extend to Rs 7500/-.

(2)Whoever-

(a)Willfully obstructs an Inspector in the discharge of his duties under this Act; or

(b)refuses or willfully neglects to afford an Inspector any reasonable facility for making any entry, inspection, examination, supervision, or inquiry authorized by or under this Act in relation to any railway, factory or industrial or other establishment; or

(c)Willfully refuses to produce on the demand of an Inspector any register or other document kept in pursuance of this Act; or

(d)prevents or attempts to prevent or does anything which he has any reason to believe is likely to prevent any person from appearing before or being examined by an Inspector acting in pursuance of his duties under this Act;

shall be punishable with fine which shall not be less than Rs 1500/- one but which may extend to Rs 7500/-.

(3)If any person who has been convicted of any offence punishable under this Act is again guilty of an offence involving contravention of the same provision, he shall be punishable on a subsequent conviction with imprisonment for a term which shall not be less than one month but which may extend to six months and with fine which shall not be less than Rs 3750/- but which may extend to Rs 22500/-.

(4)If any person fails or willfully neglects to pay the wages of any employed person by the date fixed by the authority in this behalf, he shall, without prejudice to any other action that may be taken against him, be punishable with an additional fine which may extend to Rs 750/- for each day for which such failure or neglect continues.

Payment in case of death of the employed person whose wages are not disbursed

Where the amount payable to an employed person as wages could not be paid on account of his

death before payment or on account of his whereabouts not being known;

(a)Be paid to the person nominated by him in this behalf.

(b)Where no such nomination has been made or where for any reasons such amount cannot be aid to the person nominated, be deposited with the prescribed authority.

MINIMUM WAGES ACT, 1948

The concept of Minimum Wages was first evolved by ILO in 1928 with reference to remuneration of workers in those industries where the, level of wages was substantially low and the labour was vulnerable to exploitation, being not well organised and having less effective bargaining power. The need for a legislation for fixation of minimum wages in India received boost after World War – II when a draft bill was considered by the Indian Labour Conference in 1945. On the recommendation of the 8th Standing Labour Committee, the Minimum Wages Bill was introduced in the Central Legislative assembly on 11.4.1946 to provide for fixation of minimum wages in certain employments. The Minimum Wages Bill was passed by the Indian Dominion Legislature and came into force on

15th March, 1948. Under the Act both State and Central Government are "Appropriate

Governments" for fixation/revision of minimum rates of wages for employments covered by the

Schedule to the Act. The minimum rates of wages also include Special Allowance (Variable Dearness Allowance) linked to Consumer Price Index Number which are revised twice a year effective from April and October. The rates of wages once fixed are revised at an interval not exceeding of five years.

The National Minimum Wage has been considered at various for a in the past. However, State/UT Governments are not unanimous on the need of a National Minimum Wage as socioeconomic conditions vary from state to state, region to region and also from industry to industry due to different geographical, topographical and agro-climatic factors. The Six Regional Minimum Wages Advisory Committees set up in 1987 to reduce regional disparities among States have been broadened and renamed as Regional Labour Ministers' Conferences.

Employer's Checklist for Minimum Wages
The employer must pay every employee wages as fixed by the Government.

(a)Wages must be paid in cash.

(b)For the fixation of minimum wages, the employment must have been in Schedule originally or added to the Schedule by a notification under Section 27 of the Act.

(c)The employer can take actual work on any day up to 9 hours in a 12 hours shift, but he must pay double the rate for any hour or part of an hour of actual work in excess of 9 hours or for more than 48 hours in any week.

(d)Once a minimum wage is fixed according to the provisions of the Act, the employer must pay to every employee engaged in a Scheduled employment, minimum wages notification for that class of employees.

(e)The employer should fix wage-period for the payment of wages at intervals not exceeding one month or such other larger period as may be prescribed.

(f)The employer should pay wages on a working day within seven days of the end of wage period or within 10 days if 1000 or more persons are employed in an establishment.

(g)The employer should pay the wages to a person discharged not later than the second working day after his discharge.

(h)Every employer should maintain a register of wages at workplace specifying the following particulars for each wage period in respect of each employed person:

i.Minimum rate of wages payable;

ii.The number of days in which overtime was worked;

iii.The gross wages;

iv.The wages actually paid and the date of payment.

(i)Every employer should get the signature or the thumb impression of every person employed on the wage book and the wage slips.

(j)The employer should exhibit at main entrance to the establishment and its offices, a notice in respect of the following in English and local language:

i.Minimum rates of wages;

ii.Abstracts of the Acts and rules made there under;

iii.Name and address of the Labour Inspector/ Asst. Commissioner of Labour etc.

The minimum wages covers all workers in the sectors agricultural, industrial and small-scale sectors.

This means:

farm labourers

landless labourers

factory workers

people working in cottage industries

Construction workers etc.

The issue of fixation of minimum wages is of primary importance in a country like India where 300 million people are employed in the informal sector with no collective bargaining power. This is 93 percent of the workers. The enactment of the Minimum Wages Act in 1948 is a landmark in the labour history of India. The Act provides for fixation of minimum wages for notified scheduled employment.

As per Government of India, for all the States, the minimum wages have been fixed at about Rs 40 to 60 per day per person, average about Rs 50 per day for 25 days per month.

There are 45 scheduled employments in the Central sphere and 1232 in the state sphere for which minimum wages have been fixed. To protect the wages against inflation they were linked to rise in the Consumer Price Index.

The variable dearness allowance (VDA) came into being in 1991 and the allowance is revised twice a year.

At present 22 states /Union Territories have these provisions. The states and Union Territories were further directed to ensure that minimum wages are not below Rs 45 per day for any scheduled employment.

Fixation of Minimum Wage Rate in India:

Minimum rate of the wages fixed or revised consists of the following:

A basic rate of wages and a special allowance, viz., cost of living allowance ;

A basic rate of wages with or without cost of living allowance and cash value of concessions for supplies of essential commodities ;

An all inclusive rate, i.e. basic rate, cost of living allowance and cash value of concessions.

The Government may fix the minimum rates of wages either by the hour, by the day, by the month or by such wage period as may be prescribed.

The minimum wage rate may be fixed at

a)Time rate,

b)Piece rate,

c)Guaranteed time rate and

d)Overtime rate.

The Act provides that different minimum wage rate may be fixed for

a)Different scheduled employments,

b)Different works in the same employment,

c)Adult, adolescent and children,

d)Different locations or

e)Male and Female.

Also, such minimum wage may be fixed by

a)An hour,

b)Day,

c)Month, or

d)Any other period as may be prescribed by the notified authority.

Norms for fixing minimum wage:
Three consumption units per earner,
Minimum food requirement of 2700 calories per average Indian adult,
Cloth requirement of 72 yards per annum per family,
Rent corresponding to the minimum area provided under the government's Industrial Housing Scheme and
Fuel, lighting and other miscellaneous items of expenditure to constitute 20 per cent of the total minimum wage
Fuel, lighting and other miscellaneous items of expenditure to constitute 20% of the total Minimum Wages,
Children education, medical requirement, minimum recreation including festivals/ceremonies and provision for old age, marriage etc. should further constitute 25% of the total minimum wage.

Cost of Living Allowance:
The minimum basic wages fixed are linked to consumer price index as a counter measure against inflation. The cost of living is set twice in a year. The Commissioner of Labour notifies the rate 1st of April and 1st of October. The rates are fixed on the basis of the average rise in the State industrial workers consumer price index numbers for half year ending December and June respectively.

Variable Dearness Allowance:
Dearness Allowance is payable to monthly, daily and piece rate earners. Every six months the respective State Governments issues the Cost of Living Index number for each and every scheduled employment.
For checking the minimum wage rate log on tohttp://www.paycheck.in/main/officialminimumwageshttp://www.paycheck.in/main/officialminimumwageshttp://www.paycheck.in/main/officialminimumwages. It gives state wise updated minimum wage rate with their effective date

EQUAL REMUNARISATION ACT (1976):
OBJECTIVE:
It provides for the equal remunarisation to the men and women of the same work or same nature of work and for the prevention of discrimination on grounds of sex against women on the matter of employment.
Wages should be equally distributed for men and women

SCOPE AND COVERAGE:
In extents to the whole of India and applies to establishments or employment notified by central government.
In the same case the exemption are special condition of female are considered in the period (maternity) in law and child birth or marriage or death.
Center and state decide weather if change is needed.

EMPLOYEE ENTITLED:
All employee in an establishment (central government notified alone it

can applied)

ADMINISTRATIVE AUTHORITY:
It is central legislation

Administration is by both central and state government in their respective spares.

ADVISORY COMMITTEE:
It is appropriated government admit advisory committee to advice with regard to extend to which women may be employed in specified establishment with the view to providing increasing employment opportunities for the women.

INSPECTORS:
The appropriate government appointed for the purpose of making an investigation in their local limit has to weather the provision of act or rules made they under being compete by the employers

Power to visit the industry and related things as like employer,work going on, mustard role, etc,

Evidence of any person is ascertained weather the role is applicable effectively and ask or examine or authority its rules

POWER TO MAKE RULES:
Central government has power to make rules and prescribe for their act and it may give desteration to the state government into the execution of the act into the state.

REMUNARISATION:
It means the basic wage or salary and any emulation what so ever payable either in cash or in kind to a person employed in respect of employees or work done in such employment if the time of contract of employment express or implied or fulfilled.

SAME WORK OR WORK OF SIMILAR NATURE:
It means work in respect of which the skill, effort, and responsibility required are the same. When performed under the similar working condition of men or women and the difference if any between the skill effort and responsibility required of the men and those required of the women are not of practical importance in relation to terms and condition of employment.

OBLIGATION OF EMPLOYER:
EQUAL WAGES FOR EQUAL WORK:
Employer should pay equal wages to men and women employees of his establishment to men and women for performing of same work or work of similar nature.

No discrimination during recruitment of employees

The employer should not make any discrimination against women while recruitment for same work or for work of similar mature.

MAINTANENCE OF REGISTERER:

Every employer should maintain   updated registrar in relation to the workers employed by him in prescribed form

The registrar contains particular such:
- Categories of workers
- Nature of work
- No. of men or women employee
- Rate of remunarisation paid etc,

RIGHTS OF THE EMPLOYEES:

Right to complaint against the employer's contravention of any provision of the act.

Right to file claim arising out of wages at rates to men and women workers of the same work.

Right to appeal against an order of authority in respect of the claim of complaints within 30 days of such order.

RIGHTS OF THE EMPLOYER:

The employer has the right to applies against an order of an authority in respect of the claim or order.

OFFENCE AND PENALITY:

- Failure to maintain the register or other documents or to produce on the demand then they will face an imprisonment for nearly 1 month or fine up to Rs.10,000 or worth.
- Failure to give an evidence or information required of him the punishment and the penalty is as mentioned above.
- Discrimination in recruitment or other payment of unequal wages then the fine is Rs.10,000 and 2 month to 1 year of experience
- Failure to carry out any direction of the government the fine is as like above mentioned.
- Failure to produce before an inspector an any registrar or document or information then the fine is of Rs.500

THE PAYMENT OF BONUS ACT, 1965:

The payment of Bonus Act provides for payment of bonus to persons employed in certain establishments of the basis of profits or on the basis of production or productivity and for matters connected therewith.

It extends to the whole of India and is applicable to every factory and to every other establishment where 20 or more workmen are employed on any day during an accounting year.

Eligibility for Bonus

Every employee receiving salary or wages upto Rs. 10,000 p.m. and engaged in any kind of work whether skilled, unskilled, managerial, supervisory etc. is entitled to bonus for every accounting year if he has worked for at least 30 working days in that year.

Where an employee has not worked for all the working days in an accounting year, the minimum bonus of one hundred rupees or, as the case may be, of sixty rupees, if such bonus is higher than 8.33 per cent, of his salary or wage for the days he has worked in that accounting year, shall be proportionately reduced.

However employees of L.I.C., Universities and Educational institutions, Hospitals, Chamber of Commerce, R.B.I., IFCI, U.T.I., IDBI, NABARD, SIDBI, Social Welfare institutions are not entitled to bonus under this Act.

Calculation for Working Days in An Accounting Year

An employee shall be deemed to have worked in an establishment in any accounting year also on the days on which--

(a)he has been laid off under an agreement or as permitted by standing orders under the Industrial Employment (Standing Orders) Act, 1946 (20 of 1946), or under the Industrial Disputes Act, 1947 (14 of 1947), or under any other law applicable to the establishment;

(b)he has been on leave with salary or wage;

(c)he has been absent due to temporary disablement caused by accident arising out of and in the course of his employment; and

(d)the employee has been on maternity leave with salary or wage, during the accounting year.

Disqualification for Bonus

Notwithstanding anything contained in the act, an employee shall be disqualified from receiving bonus, if he is dismissed from service for fraud or riotous or violent behaviour while in the premises of the establishment or theft, misappropriation or sabotage of any property of the establishment.

Minimum and Maximum Bonus Payable
Minimum Bonus

The minimum bonus which an employer is required to pay even if he suffers losses during the accounting year or there is no allocable surplus is 8.33 % of the salary or wages during the accounting year, or

Rs. 100 in case of employees above 15 years and Rs 60 in case of employees below 15 years, at the beginning of the accounting year, whichever is higher

Maximum Bonus

If in an accounting year, the allocable surplus, calculated after taking into account the amount 'set on' or the amount 'set of' exceeds the minimum bonus, the employer should pay bonus in proportion to the salary or wages earned by the employee in that accounting year subject to a maximum of 20% of such salary or wages.

Time Limit for Payment

The bonus should be paid in cash within 8 months from the close of the accounting year or within one month from the date of enforcement of the award or coming into operation of a settlement following an industrial dispute regarding payment of bonus.

However if there is sufficient cause extension may be applied for

Calculation of Bonus

The method for calculation of annual bonus is as follow:
1.Calculate the gross profit in the manner specified in-

a.First Schedule, in case of a banking company, or

b.Second Schedule, in any other case.

2.Calculate the Available Surplus.

Available Surplus = A+B, where A = Gross Profit – Depreciation admissible u/s 32 of the Income tax Act - Development allowance - Direct taxes payable for the accounting year (calculated as per Sec.7) – Sums specified in the Third Schedule.

B = Direct Taxes (calculated as per Sec. 7) in respect of gross profits for the immediately preceding accounting year – Direct Taxes in respect of such gross profits as reduced by the amount of bonus, for the immediately preceding accounting year.

3.Calculate Allocable Surplus

Allocable Surplus = 60% of Available Surplus, 67% in case of foreign companies.

4.Make adjustment for 'Set-on' and 'Set-off'. For calculating the amount of bonus in respect of an accounting year, allocable surplus is computed after considering the amount of set on and set off from the previous years, as illustrated in Fourth Schedule.

5.The allocable surplus so computed is distributed amongst the employees in proportion to salary or wages received by them during the relevant accounting year.

In case of an employee receiving salary or wages above Rs. 3,500 the bonus payable is to be calculated as if the salary or wages were Rs. 3,500 p.m. only.

Duties / Rights of Employer

Duties

To calculate and pay the annual bonus as required under the Act

To submit an annul return of bonus paid to employees during the year, in Form D, to the Inspector, within 30 days of the expiry of the time limit specified for payment of bonus.

To co-operate with the Inspector, produce before him the registers/records maintained, and such other information as may be required by them.

To get his account audited as per the directions of a Labour Court/Tribunal or of any such other authority.

Rights

An employer has the following rights:

Right to forfeit bonus of an employee, who has been dismissed from service for fraud, riotous or violent behaviour, or theft, misappropriation or sabotage of any property of the establishment.

Right to make permissible deductions from the bonus payable to an employee, such as, festival/interim bonus paid and financial loss caused by misconduct of the employee.

Right to refer any disputes relating to application or interpretation of any provision of the Act, to the Labour Court or Labour Tribunal.

Rights of Employees

Right to claim bonus payable under the Act and to make an application to the Government, for the recovery of bonus due and unpaid, within one year of its becoming due.

Right to refer any dispute to the Labour Court/Tribunal Employees, to whom the Payment of Bonus Act does not apply, cannot raise a dispute regarding bonus under the Industrial Disputes Act.

Right to seek clarification and obtain information, on any item in the accounts of the establishment.

Recovery of Bonus Due

Where any bonus is due to an employee by way of bonus, employee or any other person authorised by him can make an application to the appropriate government for recovery of the money due.

If the government is satisfied that money is due to an employee by way of bonus, it shall issue a certificate for that amount to the collector who then recovers the money.

Such application shall be made within one year from the date on which the money became due to the employee.

However the application may be entertained after a year if the applicant shows that there was sufficient cause for not making the application within time.

Offences and Penalties

For contravention of the provisions of the Act or rules the penalty is imprisonment upto 6 months or fine up to Rs.1000, or both.

For failure to comply with the directions or requisitions made the penalty is imprisonment upto 6 months or fine up to Rs.1000, or both.

In case of offences by companies, firms, body corporate or association of individuals, its director, partner or a principal officer responsible for the conduct of its business, as the case may be, shall be deemed to be guilty of that offence and punished accordingly, unless the person concerned proves that the offence was committed without his knowledge or that he exercised all due diligence.

UNIT IV:

Industrial housing and workers education – concept of industrial housing – importance – housing condition of industrial cities in India – problem of housing – effect, remedial measures – difference housing schemes – role of HUDCO – Tamilnadu housing board – Tamilnadu clearance board – 3 tire system of housing scheme – promotion of housing colonies – concept of workers education – meaning, scope, need, objectives, schemes of workers education – role of central board for education – role of productivity council – social security legislation

HOUSING

- Provision of comfortable shelter.
- It would keep the worker fit and cheerful for all the days in the year.

IMPORTANCE
1. It is one of the essential requirements of human being.
2. Environment plays a major role in man's health and well being.
3. Industrial unrest – The Royal commission on labour – realized – outcome – industrial housing.
4. Labour investigation committee – bad housing condition – low standard of living.
5. ILO – recommendation (no.115) – need of housing.
6. Improvement of housing condition – leads – reduced sickness, disease, absenteeism, labour turnover.

HOUSING CONDITIONS IN INDUSTRIAL CITIES IN INDIA
BOMBAY
- Working class dwelling – "chawal". It is constructed by Government, Municipal corporation, the port trust, textile mills, private landlords.
- It consist common veranda and one room.

Calcutta
- workers lived in Darks, Damp, Leaky Huts – BUSTEES.
- These huts were constructed without any proper plan. The negative features of this huts are   ill ventilated, never cleaned, contaminated water for domestic purpose, inadequate sanitation facility.

Madras
- worker lived in single room with or without veranda – "cherries"
- there is no means for rain proof, proper sanitation.

Jamshedpur
- Tata Iron &steel company – quarters – workers.
- It consist rooms, veranda, separate kitchen, proper latrines with flush type, sufficient lighting, proper ventilation.

DIFFERENT HOUSING SCHEMES
- The integrated subsided housing scheme for industrial works and economically weaker sections of the community. (1952)
- The law of income group housing scheme. (1954)
- The subsidised housing scheme for plantation workers. (1956)
- The slum clearance improvements scheme (1956)
- The village housing project scheme (1957)
- The middle income group housing scheme (1959).

- Rental housing scheme for state government employees. (1959)
- The land aquistion and development scheme (1959)
- Rural house sites – cum – hut Construction scheme for landless workers. (1971)

HUDCO

Housing and Urban Development Corporation Ltd. (HUDCO) is a public sector enterprise fully owned by the Government of India, under the Companies Act 1956. HUDCO was incorporated on 25th April, 1970.

HUDCO's objectives.

• To provide long term finance for construction of houses for residential purposes or finance or undertake housing and urban development programmes in the country;

• To finance or undertake, wholly or partly, the setting up of new or satellite towns;

• To subscribe to the debentures and bonds to be issued by the State Housing (and/ or Urban   Development) Boards, Improvement Trusts, Development Authorities etc.; specifically for the purpose of financing housing and urban development programmes;

• To finance or undertake the setting up of industrial enterprises of building material;

• To administer the moneys received, from time to time, from the Government of India and other sources as grants or otherwise for the purposes of financing or undertaking housing and urban development programmes in the country .

• To promote, establish, assist, collaborate and provide consultancy services for the projects of designing and planning of works relating to Housing and Urban Development programmes in India and abroad.

Mission

To promote sustainable habitat development to enhance quality of life.

Vision

To be among the world's leading knowledge hubs and financial facilitating organizations for habitat development.

Is HUDCO a Housing Finance Company (HFC) and if so who is the regulator of HUDCO?

Yes, HUDCO is a Housing Finance Company registered with National Housing Bank (NHB), which was established under the Act of Parliament to operate as a principal agency to promote housing finance institutions both at local and regional levels and to act as the Regulator of Housing Finance Companies.

What is the Resource Base of HUDCO?

HUDCO was established with an equity base of Rs.2 crores. Over the years, the equity base has been expanded by the Government. The present authorised capital base of HUDCO is Rs.2500 crores and paid up capital is Rs. 2001.90 crores.

Projects & Programmes of HUDCO

HUDCO extends assistance benefiting the masses in urban and rural areas under a broad spectrum of programmes as listed below:

• Urban Housing
• Rural Housing
• Staff Rental Housing
• Repairs and Renewals
• Shelter and Sanitation Facilities for Footpath dwellers in Urban Areas (Night Shelter and Pay & Use toilets)
• Working Women Ownership Condominium Housing
• Housing through Private Builders/Joint Sector
• Individual Housing Loans through 'HUDCO Niwas'
• Land Acquisition
• Jawahar Lal Nehru National Urban Renewal Mission (JNNURM)

Infrastructure
• Integrated Land Acquisition and Development
• Environmental Improvement of Slums
• Utility Infrastructure
• Social Infrastructure
• Economic and Commercial Infrastructure

Building Technology
• Building Centres for Technology Transfer at the Grass-roots
• Building Material Industries

Consultancy Services
• Consultancy in Housing, Urban Development and Infrastructure
Research And Training
• Capacity Building and Technical Assistance to all Borrowing Agencies, Research Training and Networking in Human Settlement Planning and Management.
Eligible borrowers for HUDCO loan assistance

Eligible borrowers are:
i) State level financing institutions / corporations
ii) Water supply and sewerage boards
iii) Development authorities
iv) State functional borrowers for housing & urban development
v) New town development borrowers
vi) Regional planning boards
vii) Improvement trusts
viii) Municipal corporations / councils
ix) Joint sector companies
x) Cooperative societies / trusts
xi) NGOs
xii) Private companies/borrowers including BOT operators, concessionaires

Various categories of projects under Housing Finance

All types of Housing projects includes:

i) Rural Housing

ii) Urban Housing

iii) Co-operative Housing

iv) Community Toilets

v) Slum Upgradation

vi) Staff Housing including Police Housing

vii) Repairs and Renewal

viii) Housing by NGOs

ix) Private Sector Housing

x) Takeout finance

xi) Land Acquisition cum Construction schemes

xii) Individual Housing

Projects that are eligible for HUDCO finance in Infrastructure sector

Construction, Augmentation and Improvement of the following:

i) Water Supply Projects

ii) Sewerage and Drainage

iii) Solid Waste Management

v) Integrated Area Development Schemes

vi) Social Infrastructure

vii) Transportation – Roads, Bridges, Bus terminals, Ports, Airports etc.

viii) Commercial / Economic Infrastructure

ix) Power – Generation, Transmission and Distribution

x) Industrial and Business Infrastructure – SEZ, Warehouses etc.

xi) Information / Communication / Entertainment (ICE)

xii) Telecom

xiii) Ecologically Appropriate Infrastructure Projects

To what extent HUDCO can finance

i) Govt. Borrowers:

The loan amount for a project may be upto 90% of the project cost subject to maximum of 15% of Net Owned Fund (NOF) of HUDCO.

ii) Private Sector Borrower

Loan amount may be upto 66% of project cost subject to maximum of 15% of NOF of HUDCO for a project/ SPV and upto 25% of NOF of HUDCO to group companies. Loan amount more than 100.00 crores will normally be sanctioned on consortium basis and a higher debt – equity ratio may also be considered in line with the lead lender.

Types of rates offered by HUDCO

HUDCO provides the following rates of interest:

i) Fixed rate of interest with 3 years reset option

ii) Floating rate of interest

Repayment options available for HUDCO loan

1. Monthly

2. Quarterly

3. Half-yearly

4. Yearly.

(For S.No. 3 & 4, the interest shall be calculated on quarterly basis)
First point of contact when applying for a loan from HUDCO

For acceptance and registering the Loan application, a Customer Relationship Officer (CRO) is available at all Regional Offices. The CRO is responsible for facilitating receipt of all project proposals (except HUDCO Niwas) within prescribed guidelines of HUDCO and ensuring availability of complete set of documents/ information required for determining eligibility and registration of schemes

Securities that Borrowers can submit for availing loan from HUDCO

State government guarantees/ Bank Guarantees/ Equitable mortgage of land and buildings/ Hypothecation of movable and immovable assets/ assignment of rights/ corporate guarantee/ personal guarantee etc. However, the security would depend on the risk involved in the project.

Main security, if some infrastructure project is taken up on BOT concept.

Mortgage of project properties is the main security for any type of projects. However, in BOT projects, if mortgage of project properties is not possible/enforceable/permissible then loan can also be secured by assignment of project contracts, license, permits, insurance policies, approvals, consents, concessions etc., Assignment of contractual rights, security rights, actionable claims, charge on TRA/Escrow and Hypothecation of Moveable Properties.

Security Coverage Ratio

The minimum-security coverage during the currency of loan should not be less than 125% for Govt. Agencies and 150% for Private Sector Agencies of total outstanding loan amount at any point of time.

Consultancy Services provided by HUDCO

HUDCO has developed proficiency in design and consultancy services and have

provided its services in the following areas:

• Architectural designs and detailed working drawings,

• Structural design, project estimates, Design of internal and external services,

• Landscape planning and design,

• Preparation of project reports and feasibility studies for housing, urban and

regional planning issues.

• Waste management projects

• Preparation of City Development Plans (CDPs), Master Plans etc.

Efforts are being made by HUDCO in disaster hit areas

HUDCO had provided its technological support in the disaster-hit areas. Pamphlets and books on Do's & Dont's on construction of houses and related matters had been distributed. Demonstration projects like Model Village & Model Basti were constructed as part of the Model Village & Model Basti schemes were executed by HUDCO.

HUDCO's role vis-à-vis JNNURM

HUDCO is one of the Appraising Agencies for BSUP projects and the only Appraising agency for all IHSDP projects under JNNURM.

HUDCO is doing for promoting cost effective building materials and technologies for Urban/Rural housing.

HUDCO contributes in promotion of appropriate, cost effective, building material and technologies for use in Housing and Infrastructure sector at grass root level through the National Network of Building Centres a scheme of MoH&UPA, Govt of India. The building centres promote innovative, cost effective, durable and aesthetic operations brought out by National level Research Development bodies such as CBRI. SERC, NEERI, RRLs, ASTRA, CSR, DA, INSWAREB, CSV and other state level institutions and work done by Laurie Baker.

Does HUDCO accept Public Deposit?
Yes, Public Deposit which means acceptance of deposits from various category of depositors excluding certain deposits like amount received from Central/State Governments/Banks/Public Financial Institutions and mutual Funds etc. are accepted by HUDCO.
Required norms to be disclosed by HUDCO in the Application Form soliciting public deposits
While accepting deposits HUDCO indicates the following in the Application
Form:
i) Particulars of eligible category of depositor.
ii) Credit rating assigned for its deposits.
iii) Particulars as required under non-banking financial companies and miscellaneous non-banking companies (Advertisement), Rules, 1977.
iv) Rate of interest and period of deposit.
v) KYC requirements
vi) Principal terms and conditions of deposit scheme.
vii) Summarize financial position of the company for the last two years balance sheet.
viii) Name of the Registered Office and its branches accepting deposits.

TAMIL NADU HOUSING BOARD
To cater the housing needs of growing population and to mitigate the hardship in getting houses or house sites and owing to urbanisation the Tamil Nadu Housing Board was established in Chennai city in 1961, with an objective of providing "Housing for All". Since its inception, Tamil Nadu Housing Board has completed 400583 Housing Units all over the state. Among the 400583 Housing Units, 125741 units are allotted for Economically weaker sections; 93254 units are allotted for Low income groups; and 72653 units are allotted for Middle income groups.

Stage of schemes
1.1Schemes under implementation
During the year 2011-12, 1305 housing units have been completed, 2178 are nearing completion and 3704 are in progress. Works on 955 units will be commenced shortly.
Interest subsidy for housing the urban poor
TNHB was appointed as nodal agency to implement the Central Government's Interest Subsidy scheme for Housing the Urban Poor (ISHUP). During this financial year, the target has been fixed for sanction of loan for 2 lakh beneficiaries. Till date, TNHB has collected about 72266

applications from the eligible persons and 55657 applications have been sent to the respective banks for sanction of loan. So far, loans were sanctioned for 4,591 eligible persons.

Government Servants

The construction works are in progress for the construction of 1016 Multi-Storied Flats at Nerkundram, Chennai at a cost of Rs.445 crore for All India Service Officers, Group I Officers and other categories of Government Officials. The construction will be completed by April 2014.

Integrated township at Thirumazhisai

It is proposed to develop an Integrated Township at a cost of Rs.2160 Crore near Thirumazhisai, Thiruvallur District, over an extent of 311.05 acres of land already acquired by the Tamil Nadu Housing Board under Public Private Partnership (PPP) Mode. Action is being taken for the acquisition to an extent of 12.87 acres required for approach road and 12.65 acres on alienation from the Government. Advisor has been appointed for preparing feasibility report and to recommend the mode of development.

Construction of 554 MSB Apartments at Wood Working Unit near Ashok Pillar

It is proposed to construct 554 MSB apartments at Wood Working Unit near Ashok Pillar at a cost of Rs.100 crore in an extent of 3.73 acres under Public Private Partnership (PPP) Mode. The project will be implemented during the current year.

Construction of Commercial Complex cum 120 MSB Flats at SAF Games Village

It is proposed to construct Commercial Complex cum 120 MSB flats at SAF Games Village at a cost of Rs.149.00 crore in an extent of 5.60 acres under Public Private Partnership (PPP) Mode. The project will be implemented during the current year.

Re-Development of Board's Rental Flats at Mandavelipakkam and C.I.T Nagar

(A) Mandavelipakkam

The reconstruction of 52 flats is proposed at a cost of Rs.11.80 crore by demolishing the existing 27 flats constructed during 1963. The project will be implemented during the current year.

(B)CIT Nagar, Nandanam

The reconstruction of 474 flats is proposed at a cost of Rs.77.70 crore by demolishing the existing

119 quarters constructed during 1959 . The project will be implemented during the current year.

Re-Construction of Tamil Nadu Government Rental Housing Flats

(A)Anna Nagar West (Thirumangalam)

It has been proposed to spend Rs.80.00 crore for the re-construction of 606 Tamil Nadu Government Rental Housing flats in the place of 126

Tamil Nadu Government Rental Housing flats at Anna Nagar west already demolished. Construction work will commence during this financial year.

(B)Foreshore Estate

It has been proposed to spend Rs.450.00 crore for the re-construction of 1610 Tamil Nadu Government Rental Housing flats at Foreshore Estate in an extent 21.03 acres in the place of 1112 Tamil Nadu Government Rental Housing flats already demolished. Construction work will commence after obtaining Coastal Regulation Zone (CRZ) clearance.

(C)Koundampalayam-Coimbatore

It has been proposed to spend Rs.450.00 crore for the construction of 2000 Tamil Nadu Government Rental Housing flats at Koundampalayam after demolishing the 1642 dilapidated Tamil Nadu Government Rental Housing flats located in 6 places at Coimbatore namely Koundampalayam, Gandhipuram, Uppilipalayam, Seeranaickenpalayam, Race Course area and District Forest Officer Compound. Construction work will commence during this financial year.

Reconstruction of Dilapidated Board Buildings

Reconstruction of shopping complex / Community hall taken up in six locations in Chennai. The existing floor area of 20095 sq.ft. will be increased to 73822 sq.ft. through reconstruction at a cost of Rs.13.29 Crore. Necessary approvals will be obtained and the construction will commence during the current year.

Issue of Sale Deeds

There are 76382 sale deeds to be given to the allottees. During the year 2011-2012 concerted efforts were taken to issue sale deeds to the allottees and 21931 sale deeds were issued. Remaining 54451 sale deed could not be given due to various reasons. Action will be taken during this year to issue remaining sale deeds. The proposals for waiver of interest and penal interest are under the consideration of the Government. Orders will be issued early.

Disposal of unsold stocks

During the year 2011-2012, 6283 Units have been sold out and Rs. 637.89 crore has been realised.

Part I Schemes

The details of various types of quarters under the maintenance of Tamil Nadu Housing Board are as follows:-

During the year 2011-2012, Rs.1774.05 lakh was allocated and works are under progress for regular maintenance of Tamil Nadu Government Rental Housing Scheme flats all over Tamil Nadu, maintenance of MLA Hostel and Subsidised Industrial Housing Scheme (SIHS) colonies.
For the year 2012-13, a Budget allocation of Rs.1096.00 lakh has been proposed for regular maintenance of Tamil Nadu Government Rental Housing Scheme flats all over Tamil Nadu, maintenance of MLA Hostel

and SIHS colonies.

Part II Schemes
During the year 2011-12, the Government have sanctioned an amount of Rs.1.40 crore for the construction of 12 TNGRHS flats at Villupuram throughPart-II Scheme and action is being taken to implement the scheme early.

WORKERS EDUCATION
Log on to http://cbwe.gov.in/http://cbwe.gov.in/ to have the information on Central Board of Worker's Education.
About CBWE
The Central Board for Workers Education (CBWE) is an autonomous body under the Ministry of Labour & Employment, Government of India. It is registered under the Societies Registration Act, 1860. Started in 1958, the Workers Education Scheme in India has been playing a very significant role in our national development; creating an enlightened and disciplined work force and bringing about desirable behavioral changes in our workforce in the organized, unorganized and rural sectors. It gets grants-in-aid from the Ministry of Labour & Employment to operate its activities. The Scheme of Workers Education aims at achieving the objectives of creating and increasing awareness and educating the workforce for their effective participation in the socio-economic development of the country. To achieve these objectives, various training programmes are conducted by the Board for the workers of formal and informal sectors at national, regional and unit levels through a network of http://www.cbwe.gov.in/Regional.asp50 Regional and 09 Sub-Regional Directorates spread all over the country and an apex Training Institute viz. http://www.cbwe.gov.in/admin_view_uniquepagesbody.asp?ID_PK=5Indian Institute of Workers Education (IIWE) at Mumbai.

http://www.cbwe.gov.in/admin_view_uniquepagesbody.asp?ID_PK=89CBWE Regional Directorates

http://www.cbwe.gov.in/admin_view_uniquepagesbody.asp?ID_PK=149Sub-Regional Directorates

Objectives of Workers Education:

- To strengthen among all sections of the working class, including rural workers, a sense of patriotism, national integrity, unity, amity, communal harmony, secularism and pride in being an Indian.

- To equip all sections of workers, including rural workers and women workers, for their intelligent participation in social and economic development of the nation in accordance with its declared objectives.

  To develop amongst the workers a greater understanding of the problems of their social and economic environment, their responsibilities towards family members, and their rights and obligations as citizens, as workers in industry and as members and officials of trade union.

  To develop capacity of workers in all aspects to meet the challenges of the country from time to time.

- To develop strong, united and more responsible trade unions and to strengthen democratic processes and traditions in the trade union movement through more enlightened members and better trained officials.

  To empower the workers as employees of the organization and to develop sense of belongingness as effective instruments of amicable industrial relations and maintaining industrial peace.
- To meet the needs of workers to have access to ways of acquiring and continuous upgradation of knowledge and skills that they require to find and hold a job.

Objectives Of Rural Workeres Education

To promote among rural workers, critical awareness of the problems of their socio-economic environment and their privileges and obligations as workers, as members of the village community and as citizens.

To educate the rural workers to enhance their self-confidence and build-up a scientific attitude.

To educate rural workers in protecting and promoting their individual and social interests.

To educate rural workers in developing their organisations through which they can fulfil socio- economic functions and responsibilities in rural economy and strenghten democratic, secular, and socialist fibre of rural society. Hence motivating rural workers for family welfare planning and to combat social evils

CENTRAL SECTOR

2.Various plan schemes of the Ministry of Labour aim at achievement of welfare and social security of the working class and maintenance of industrial peace. As against the approved outlay of Rs.130 crore for the year 1999-2000, the anticipated expenditure would be Rs.104 crore. The approved outlay for the year 2000-2001 is Rs.123 crore. (Refer Annexure 5.7.1 for Central Sector and Annexure 5.7.2 for State sector).

3.Plan initiatives in the Labour & Labour Welfare Sector are as under:

(i)Training for skill development.

(ii)Services to job seekers.

(iii)Welfare of labour.

(iv)Administration of labour regulations.

4.Under the Constitution of India, Vocational Training is a concurrent subject. The development of training schemes at National level, evolution of policy, laying of training standards, procedures, conducting of examinations, certification, etc. are the responsibility of the Central Government, where as the implementation of the training schemes largely rests with the State/U.T. governments. The Central Government is advised by the National Council of Vocational Training (NCVT), a tripartite body which has representation from employers, workers and Central/State governments. At the State level, similar councils known as State Councils for Vocational Training are constituted for the same purpose by the respective state governments at state levels.

5.The main objectives of the scheme are as under:

(i)To ensure steady flow of skilled workers.

(ii)To raise the quality and quantity of industrial production by systematic training of potential workers.

(iii)To reduce unemployment among educated youth by equipping them with suitable skills for industrial employment.

6.The main Vocational Training Schemes comprise of Craftsmen Training Scheme, Apprenticeship Training Scheme, Training of skilled workers, training of women as a special target group, Training of Craft Instructors, Training of Supervisors and also to carry out applied research on vocational training problems while paying adequate attention towards preparation and development of instructional material.

7.The Craftsmen Training Scheme and Apprenticeship Training Scheme which are adequately dovetailed and meant to bring maximum benefit to the youth in their formative years, form the centre stage of the vocational training schemes. A number of other departments have also started training activities for their respective sectors e.g. Small Industry, KVIC, handlooms, tourism (hotel management & catering), electronics, medical technicians, agriculture and rural development. These training schemes are smaller but serve a very useful and essential purpose in the overall sphere of vocational training. In spite of difficulties ·and shortcomings, the Vocational Training Schemes have continued to make progress especially in terms of being the primary source of manpower for the industry.

8.The Central Government mainly concentrates on laying down the policies, procedures and training standards while the management of ITIs are under the concerned State Government(s)/U.Ts. In this process, the Central Government is advised by two
tripartite advisory bodies namely, the National Council for Vocational Training (NCVT) and the Central Apprenticeship Council (CAC). Both the Councils have the Union Labour Minister as the Chairman. Annual meeting of the two bodies was held in the month of July, 1999. In the meeting the steps to improve the quality of training both under NCVT and CAC were discussed and concrete recommendations emerged. The following are the important recommendations:

·Setting up an Expert group to look into the issues relating to Vocational Training Programme for persons with disability (equal opportunities under the persons with Disability Act, 1995) and its implementation under CTS.
·Introduction of four new trades viz. Computer Hardware, Medical Electronics, Consumer Electronics and Industrial Electronics under CTS.
·Revision of space norms for workshops.
·Introduction of modular training for advanced skill courses for women at NVTI/RVTIs under DGE&T.

CRAFTSMEN TRAINING SCHEME

9.The Craftsmen Training Scheme (CTS) under the National Vocational Training System was introduced in 1950 for imparting skill training. Training is imparted mainly in engineering trades. A few trades outside the engineering field are also covered but the bulk of the services sector and need of industries other than manufacturing are not handled by DGE&T. In the area of training, six new trades (in the areas of Information Technology, Electronics) in Craftsmen Training Scheme in different ITIs and nine new trades under Apprenticeship Training Scheme have been introduced.

10.There has been a significant growth and expansion in the network of ITIs which have grown to 4172 in the Public and Private sectors with a seating capacity of 6.78 lakh as on 31.12.99(State-wise details presented in Annexure 5.7.3) and another 2.33 lakh under the Trade Apprentice Scheme. The Apprenticeship Training Scheme provides practical training

Labour and Labour Welfare

in 137 designated trades to train apprentices in 101 subject fields in engineering and technology for graduates and diploma holders and 94 subject fields for technicians. Details of Region wise utilisation in respect of Trade Apprentices in the Central Sector and State Sectors as on 30.6.99 are given in Annexures 5.7.4 & 5.7.5.

11.Directorate General of Employment and Training, through its women's occupational Training Directorate, launched the women's Vocational

Training Programme in 1977. The programme aimed at providing Vocational Training facilities to women, thereby increasing their employability and consequently their participation in the economy of the country. Under the Vocational Training Programme at Central Sector, training facilities for women in Vocational Skills are being provided through a network of Women's Vocational Training Institutes.

12.The Government has initiated steps for strengthening and modernisation of Industrial Training Institutes (ITIs) in Jammu & Kashmir. All trades that have demand and local relevance will be covered by including even such activities that are presently outside NCVT approved trades such as construction, carpet weaving, horticulture, catering, tourism, etc.

13.The existing training institutions have, no doubt, been meeting a significant part of the requirements of the skilled manpower of the organised industry. It, however, seems necessary that the process of restructuring and reorientation of their courses is expedited with a view to quickly responding to the labour market. For skill upgradation of the workers in the unorganised sector, flexibility in the duration, training and location of training courses would need to be introduced. To the extent a sizeable proportion of employment would have to be self employment in tiny and small units in various sectors, the training system should also gear up not only for providing hard skills for suitable trades, but also the soft skills of entrepreneurship, management and marketing, as part of training courses.

14.In order to improve accessibility to employment to trainees from ITIs, there is need to take up a new market driven trades and dispense with the traditional trades such as blacksmith, carpentry, conventional tailoring etc. Since the ITIs are being run by the States, the State Governments have been advised to network with the industry and bring changes in their syllabus/trades of ITIs. In this direction, some of the States have already taken steps, for example, the State Government of Haryana is opening up an ITI in Gurgaon in collaboration with Confederation of Indian Industry. The trades/syllabus are being decided in consultation with the CII keeping in view the future demands of the industry. The financial burden will also be shared by the industry. The Government of Gujarat has also started networking with the industry in the change over of obsolete trades to make them market driven.

NATIONAL EMPLOYMENT SERVICE

15. National Employment Service covers all the States and Union Territories except Sikkim, and functions within the framework of the Employment Exchanges (compulsory notification of vacancies) Act 1959. Day to Day administration of the Employment Exchanges is with the State/U.T. governments. It has a network of 953 Employment Exchanges as on 30.6.99. Year-wiseregistration, placement, vacancies notified, submission made and live register for the period 1989 to 1998 may be seen in Annexure 5.7.6. The main activities of the Employment Exchanges are registration, placement of job seekers, career

counselling, vocational guidance and collection of labour market information. Special self employment promotion cells (SEPCs) have been established in 23 selected Employment Exchanges up to the end of December, 1998, 0.7 lakh persons have been placed in self employment and 1.8 lakh persons were on the live register of these cells seeking self employment assistance.

16.National Employment Service in the context of newly emerging market scenario has to be reoriented. The Employment Services has now accepted its enhanced role and is paying greater attention to compilation and dissemination of comprehensive labour market information. The important reports generated by the Employment Market Information Programme are "The Quarterly Employment Review", "Occupational and Educational Pattern in India", etc. There are also plan schemes for modernisation and computerisation of employment exchanges for strengthening of Employment Market information programme.

17.The Employment service continued to pay special attention to the needs of the weaker section of society. A comprehensive package of services is provided to the handicapped by 17 vocational rehabilitation centres for the handicapped. Out of these, the Vocational Rehabilitation Centre at Vadodara has been set up exclusively for disabled women. These centres evaluate the residual capacities of the handicapped and provide them adjustment training, facilitating their early economic rehabilitation. Efforts are also made to assist them in obtaining other suitable rehabilitation services such as job placement and training for self-employment. Setting up of seven new Vocational Rehabilitation Centres (VRCS), 12 skill Training workshops in the Vocational Rehabilitation Centres and 26 Rural Rehabilitation Extension Centres is under consideration of the Ministry of Labour. Vocational guidance and training in confidence building is provided to job seekers belonging to the scheduled castes and the scheduled tribes at 22 coaching-cum-guidance centres. In addition, the scheme to provide facilities to SCs/STs job seekers for practicing shorthand and typing is in operation in Coaching-cum-guidance (CGCs).

SOCIAL SECURITY LEGISLATION

here are also laws enacted and schemes established by the Central/State Governments providing for social security and welfare of specific categories of working people. The principal social security laws enacted centrally are the following:

- ·The Workmen's Compensation Act, 1923.
- ·The Employees State Insurance Act, 1948.

Labour and Labour Welfare

·The Employees Provident Funds and Miscellaneous Provisions Act, 1953.

- ·The Maternity Benefit Act, 1961.
- ·The Payment of Gratuity Act, 1972.

.The E.P.F. & M.P. Act is administered exclusively by the Government of India through the EPFO. The cash benefits under the ESI are administered by the Central Government through the Employees State Insurance Corporation (ESIC) whereas medical care under the ESI Act is being administered by the State Governments and Union Territory Administrations. The Payment of Gratuity Act is administered by the Central Government in establishments under its control, establishments having branches in more than one State, major ports, mines, oil fields and the railways and by the State Governments and Union Territory Administrations in all other cases. In mines and circus industry, the provisions of the Maternity Benefit Act are being administered by the Central Government through the Chief Labour Commissioner (Central) and by the State Governments in factories, plantation and other establishments. The provisions of the Workmen's compensation Act are being administered exclusively by State Governments.

Employees Pension Scheme, 1995 was amended in February, 1999 to provide for pension to dependent father/mother in respect of a deceased member, who has no eligible family members and if no nomination was executed by him during his life time. Permanent and totally disabled children of the PF members were made entitled w.e.f. February, 1999 to payment of monthly children/orphan pension irrespective of age and number of children in the family. Disbursement of pension and provident fund benefits on the date of retirement in Public Sector Undertaking and model private sector establishment was introduced. One hundred and thirty six beneficiaries were paid benefits on the date of retirement during the two months December 1998 and January, 1999. Under the Workmen Compensation Act, persons employed as cooks in hotels/restaurants made eligible for benefits of compensation w.e.f. July, 1998.

For workers of poor families not covered under any insurance scheme or any law statute, the Central Government has introduced a scheme of Personal Accident Insurance Social Security Scheme. The Scheme is applicable to all persons in the age group of 18-55 who are earning members of poor families and meet with fatal accidents. The quantum of benefits is Rs.3,000. The Scheme is implemented through the General Insurance Corporation.

A new initiative has been taken by the Ministry of Agriculture and Cooperation by providing insurance cover to unorganised labour working in construction industry, agriculture fields and forests where the insurance cover will be provided through the Co-operatives on 50:50 basis through the national insurance cover and Labour Co-operatives. A premium of Rs.5.25 per annum will be paid by the Co-operatives. The insurance cover has the provision that in the case of death of a labourer, his family will be paid Rs.25,000

UNIT V:
Employee state insurance act
Employee's provident fund and miscellaneous profusions act.
Provident fund/ public provident fund.
Employees deposit linked insurance scheme 1976
Employees pension scheme1995.
Payment of gratuity act 1972 – TN payment of subsistence act 1981 –

TN conferment of permanent status act 1981 – workmen's compensation act 1923.

EMPLOYEE STATE INSURANCE ACT, 1948

The Employee State Insurance Act, [ESIC] 1948, is a piece of social welfare legislation enacted primarily with the object of providing certain benefits to employees in case of sickness, maternity and employment injury and also to make provision for certain others matters incidental thereto. The Act in fact tries to attain the goal of socio-economic justice enshrined in the Directive principles of state policy under part 4 of our constitution, in particular articles 41, 42 and 43 which enjoin the state to make effective provision for securing, the right to work, to education and public assistance in cases of unemployment, old age, sickness and disablement. The act strives to materialize these avowed objects through only to a limited extent. This act becomes a wider spectrum than factory act. In the sense that while the factory act concerns with the health, safety, welfare, leave etc of the workers employed in the factory premises only. But the benefits of this act extend to employees whether working inside the factory or establishment or elsewhere or they are directly employed by the principal employee or through an intermediate agency, if the employment is incidental or in connection with the factory or establishment.

Related Legislations: ESI (Central) Rules, 1950 and ESI (General) Regulations, 1950

Origin

The Employee State Insurance act was promulgated by the Parliament of India in the year 1948.To begin with the ESIC scheme was initially launched on 2nd February 1952 at just two industrial centers in the country namely Kanpur and Delhi with a total coverage of about 1.20 lakh workers. There after the scheme was implemented in a phased manner across the country with the active involvement of the state governments.

Objectives:

The ESI Act is a social welfare legislation enacted with the object of providing certain benefits to employees in case of sickness, maternity and employment injury. Under the Act, employees will receive medical relief, cash benefits, maternity benefits, pension to dependents of deceased workers and compensation for fatal or other injuries and diseases

.

Definitions

According to Section 2 (m) of Factories Act, 1948, Factory means any premises including the precincts thereof -

(a)whereon ten or more persons are employed or were employed for wages on any day of the preceding twelve months, and in any part of which a manufacturing process is being carried on with the aid of power or is ordinarily so carried on, or

(b)whereon twenty or more persons are employed or were employed for wages on any day of the preceding twelve months, and in any part of which a manufacturing process is being carried on without the aid of power or is ordinarily so carried on.

but does not include a mine subject to the operation of Mines Act, 1952 or a railway running shed;

According to Section 2 (k) of Factories Act, "manufacturing process" means any process for - (i) making, altering, repairing, ornamenting, finishing, packing, oiling, washing, cleaning, breaking up, demolishing, or otherwise treating or adapting any article or substance with a view to its use, sale, transport, delivery or disposal, or

(ii)pumping oil, water, sewage or any other substance; or;

(iii)generating, transforming or transmitting power; or

(iv)composing types for printing, printing by letter press, lithography, photogravure or other similar process or book binding; Ira-6] [Ira-7 or Ira-7]

(v)constructing, reconstructing, repairing, refitting, finishing or breaking up ships or vessels;

(vi)preserving or storing any article in cold storage;

According to Section 2 (h) of The Minimum Wages Act, "wages"- means all remuneration capable of being expressed in terms of money which would if the terms of the contract of employment express or implied were fulfilled be payable to a person employed in respect of his employment or of work done in such employment and includes house rent allowance but does not include -

(i) the value of -

(a)any house accommodation supply of light water medical attendance or

(b)any other amenity or any service excluded by general or special order of the appropriate government;

(ii)any contribution paid by the employer to any person fund or provident fund or under any scheme of social insurance;

(iii)any traveling allowance or the value of any traveling concession;

(iv)any sum paid to the person employed to defray special expenses entailed on him by the nature of his employment; or

(v)any gratuity payable on discharge

Applicability:

The ESI Act extends to the whole of India.

It applies to all the factories including Government factories (excluding seasonal factories), which employ 10 or more employees and carry on a manufacturing process with the aid of power and 20 employees where manufacturing process is carried out without the aid of power.

The act also applies to shops and establishments. Generally, shops and establishments employing more than 20 employees are covered by the Act. "Shop" according to the Delhi Shops and Establishment Act, 1954 means any premises where goods are sold either by

retail or wholesale or where services are rendered to customers, and includes an office, astore-room, godown, warehouse or workhouse or work place, whether in the same premises or otherwise, used in or in connection with such trade or business but does not include a factory or a commercial establishment. "Establishment" means a shop, a commercial establishment, residential hotel, restaurant, eating-house, theatre or other places of public amusement or entertainment to which this Act applies and includes such other establishment as Government may, by notification in the Official Gazette, declare to be an establishment for the purpose of this Act. According to the Delhi Shops and Establishment

Act, 1954, "Commercial Establishment" means any premises wherein any trade, business or profession or any work in connection with, or incidental or ancillary thereto is carried on and includes a society registered under the Societies Registration Act, 1860, and charitable or other trust, whether registered or not, which carries on any business, trade or profession or work in connection with, or incidental or ancillary thereto, journalistic and printing establishments, contractors and auditors establishments, quarries and mines not governed by the Mines Act, 1952, educational or other institutions run for private gain, and premises in which business of banking, insurance, stocks and shares, brokerage or produce exchange is carried on, but does not include a shop or a factory registered under the Factories Act, 1948, or theatres, cinemas, restaurants, eating houses, residential hotels, clubs or other places of public amusements or entertainment. Form 01 – Employers' Registration Form also requires a copy of the registration certificate or licence obtained under the Shops and Establishment Act to be attached along with this form. From this it is quite evident that ESI Act will be applicable to shops and establishments. Again the definition of shops and establishment will vary from state to state depending on the shops and establishment act of that particular state.

The act does not apply to any member of Indian Naval, Military or Air Forces.

All employees including casual, temporary or contract employees drawing wages less than Rs 10,000 per month are covered. The ceiling limit has been raised from Rs.7500 to Rs.10000 with effect from 01.10.06.

Apprentices covered under the Apprenticeship Act are not covered under this Act. According to Apprenticeship Act 1961, "apprentice" means a person who is undergoing apprenticeship training in pursuance of a contract of apprenticeship.

o The apprentices under any scheme as the name suggests come to learn the tricks of the trade and may not count much so far as the output of the factory is concerned, with that end in view, the apprentices are exempted from the operation of laws

relating to labour unless the State Government thought otherwise.-- Regional

Director ESIC v. M/s Arudyog 1987 (1) LLJ 292.

A factory or establishment, to which this Act applies, shall continue to be governed by its provisions even if the number of workers employed falls below the specified limit or the manufacturing process therein ceases to be carried on with the aid of power subsequently.

Where a workman is covered under the ESI scheme,

oCompensation under the Workmen's Compensation Act cannot be claimed in respect of employment injury.

o No benefits can be claimed under the Maternity Benefits Act.

Important Case laws

1.Where by some club not only sporting facilities but a kitchen is also maintained, wherein a big number of members come, it is not necessary that they are participating only in sports activities, they are also entertaining themselves and their guests by partaking beverages and tea served by the club. Activity in the kitchen has a direct connection with the activities carried on in the rest of the club premises. It is necessary that the club be registered under ESI Act as regards all the employees engaged by the club irrespective of the fact in which department they are working. Cricket Club of India satisfies the definition of the term `factory' under s. 2(12) of the Act hence covered by it.-- Cricket Club of India v. ESI Corporation 1994 (69) FLR 19.

2.Where in an establishment activities like that of clearing and forwarding is going on, it would fall within the expression "shop" even though clearing of documents is done in customs house meant for export and import of goods. Person involved in such business is catering to the needs of exporters and importers and others wanting to carry the goods further. -- AIR 1993 SC 252 .

3.Anyone having product may approach advertising agency. The advertising agency will prepare an advertising campaign for him utilising the services of the experts it employs in this behalf. It sells the campaign to the client and receives the price thereof. Indubitably, the price will depend upon the nature of the campaign but that does not make any great difference. Essentially, the advertising agency sells its expert services to a client to enable the client to launch an effective campaign of his products without staining the language, the premises of an advertising agency can be said to be a "shop"--ESICorporation v. R.K. Swamy 1993 (67) FLR 1145 : 1993 (2) CLR 1068.

4.Where a laid-off employee after signing the lay-off register was coming out of the factory premises and when crossing the road was hit by a scooter, injuries sustained by him were taken as covered during the course of employment on the basis of theory of notional extension.-- Satya Sharma v. ESI Corporation 1991 (63) FLR 339 .

5.If the work by the employee is conducted under the immediate gaze or overseeing of the principal employer or his agent, subject to other conditions as envisaged being fulfilled he would be an employee for the purpose of s. 2(9).-- CES Corporation Ltd. v. Subash Chandra Bose 1992 (1) LLJ 475.

6.A work that is conducive to the work of the factory or establishment or that is necessary for the augmentation of the work of the factory or establishment will be incidental or preliminary to or connected with the work of the factory or establishment. The casual employees shall also be brought within it and are entitled to the benefits which the Act grants. The casual labour employed to construct additional buildings for expansion of the factory are the employees under the Act.-- Regional Director, ESIC v. South India Flour Mills Ltd. 1986 (53) FLR 178.

7.Employees engaged for repairs, site clearing, construction of buildings, etc. of the principal employer are employees within the meaning of s.

2(9) of the Act. --KirloskarPneumatic Co. Ltd. v. ESI Corporation 1987 (70) FJR 199.

8.The expression "employed for wages or in connection with the work of a factory or establishment" is of very wide amplitude and its generality is not in any way prejudiced by the expression and includes any person employed for wages or any work connected with the administration of the factory or establishment or in connection with sale or distribution of the products of the factory or establishments. The word "includes" in the statutory definition of a term is generally used to enlarge the meaning of the preceding words and it is by way of extension and not with restriction. In order to determine whether the employees of the company working at its branch sales offices and carrying on acts of sale and distribution of goods manufactured by the company as well as the goods produced by the foreign company are "employees" what is pertinent is not whether they are "principally" and primarily engaged in sale and distribution of the products of the company but whether the business of sale and distribution either "principally" or "marginally" of the products of the foreign company is being done on behalf of the company. If the main business of the company itself at the branch sales offices, is to sell and distribute products of foreign company and the employees working have been employed by the company basically in connection with this work, it would be difficult to hold that the employees at branch sales offices are not "employees" within the meaning of the term defined in s. 2(9) of the Act notwithstanding the fact that the sale and distribution of the products of the company at

such offices are only marginal.-- Director General, ESI Corporation v. Scientific Instrument Co.

Ltd. 1995 Lab. IC 651 .

9.Where the work of fixing the marble is extended to a contractor by a marble manufacturing company, duty of the contractor is only to complete the work while marble, cement etc., is supplied by the manufacturing company, workers employed by the contractor would be the employees of the factory as under s. 2(9) of the Act.-- 1992 (2) CLR 881.

10.There is no such difference as that of casual or temporary or permanent employee for the expression "employee" as defined under s. 2(9) of the Act. It is so wide as to include even a casual employee who is employed just for a day for wages. The test being whether the person is employed for wages on any work which is connected with the work of a factory or establishment which bears the application of the Act except those exempted by thedefinition.-- ESI Corporation v. Suvarna Saw Mills 1980 (57) FJR 154.

11.Where a department of publication and press run by the university concerned is engaged in the printing of text books, journals, registers, forms, etc., that would amount to manufacturing process.-- Osmania University v. ESI Corporation 1986 (1) LLN 72 .

12.Where there was no manufacturing of articles nor the hotel was manufacturing any article with the aid of power except maintaining one refrigerator to preserve milk and curd, and as there was no using of power in the kitchen for making the eatables and the refrigerator had been kept only for preservation of milk and curd, there was no manufacturingprocess.-- Ritz Hotel v. ESI Corpn. 1995 (1) Mah. LJ 63.

13.Wages paid for the holidays are wages as defined.-- R.D., ESI Corporation v. Raj Keshaw Co. 1991 Lab. IC 1991 Lab. IC 1989.

14.Overtime wages could not be treated as "wages" for the purpose of contribution under the Act.-- Hind Art Press v. ESI Corporation 1990 (1) LLJ 195.

15.The ESI Corporation is conferred with the power to recover arrears of contributions from the employer along with damages/interest on the contribution that remained due. Correspondingly it is under an obligation to pay with interest the arrears of benefits to the insured employees or his dependents.-- ESI Corporation v. Bhag Singh 1989 (2) LLJ 126.

16.Section 53 of the ESI Act (Bar against receiving or recovery of compensation or damages under any other law) does not bar the remedy under s. 110A of the Motor Vehicles Act,1939.-- Deputy General Manager KSRTC v. Gopal Mudaliar 1983 (46) FLR 194.

Areas Covered
The ESI Scheme is being implemented area-wise by stages. The Scheme is being implemented in almost all union territories and states except Nagaland, Manipur, Tripura, Sikkim, Arunachal Pradesh and Mizoram.

Administration of the Act
The provisions of the Act are administered by the Employees State Insurance Corporation. It comprises members representing employees, employers, the central and state government, besides, representatives of parliament and medical profession. A standing committee constituted from amongst the members of the corporation, acts as an executive body. The medical benefit council, constituted by the central government, is another statutory body that advises the corporation on matters regarding administration of medical benefit, the certification for purposes of the grant of benefits and other connected matters.

Registration
The employer should get his factory or establishment registered with the ESI Corporation within 15 days after the Act becomes applicable to it and also obtain the employer's code number. Application should be made in Form 01 and after having being satisfied with the application form, the regional office will allot a code number to the employer, which must be quoted in all documents and correspondence.

Identity Card
An employee is required to file a declaration form upon employment in factory or establishment to show that he is covered under the Act.

On registration every insured person is provided with a 'temporary identification certificate' which is valid ordinarily for a period of three months but may be extended, if necessary, for a further period of 3 months. Within this period, the insured person is given a permanent 'family photo identity card' in exchange for the certificate. The identity card serves as a means of identification and has to be produced at the time of claiming medical care at the dispensary / clinic and cash benefit at the local office of the corporation. In the event of change of employment, it should be produced before the new employer as evidence of registration under the scheme to prevent any duplicate registration. The identity card bears the signature/thumb impression of the insured person. Since medical benefit is also available to the families of Insured persons, the particulars of family members entitled to medical benefit are also given in the identity card affixed with a postcard size family photo. If the identity card is lost, a duplicate card is issued on payment as prescribed.

Employers' / Employees' Contribution

Like most of the social security schemes, the world over, ESI scheme is a self-financing health insurance scheme. Contributions are raised from covered employees and their employers as a fixed percentage of wages. Presently covered employees contribute 1.75% of the wages, whereas as the employers contribute 4.75% of the wages, payable to the insured persons. Employees earning less than and up to Rs. 50 per day are exempted from payment of contribution.

The contribution is deposited by the employer in cash or by cheque at the designated branches of some nationalized banks. The responsibility for payment of all contributions is that of the employer with a right to deduct the employees share of contribution from employees' wages relating to the period in respect of which the contribution is payable.

There are two contribution periods each of six months duration and two corresponding benefit periods. Cash benefits under the scheme are generally linked with contribution paid.

Contribution period - 1st April to 30th September, its corresponding Cash Benefit period is 1st January to 30th June of the following year.

Contribution period - 1st October to 31st March, its corresponding Cash Benefit period is 1st July to 31st December of the following year.

Certification of Return of Contribution by Auditor

Regulation 26 of Employees' State Insurance (General) Regulations, 1950 was amended by

Notification No.N-12/13/1/2008-P&D to include certain details to be mentioned in the Return of Contribution to be submitted by employers. The salient features of amendments made in the Returns of Contribution are as under:-

1.Self-declaration by Employers regarding maintenance of records and registers, submission of Declaration Forms, employees engaged directly or through immediate employers and wages paid to the workers.

2.All the Employers employing 40 and more employees shall have to append a certificate duty certified by a Chartered Accountant, in the revised format of Returns of Contribution.

3.The Employers employing less than 40 employees will have to provide self- certification

without any certification from the Chartered Accountants in Return of Contribution.

The Chartered Accountant should certify that he has verified the return from the records and registers of the company.

This notification has come into force with effect from 01-04-2008.

Benefits under the Scheme

Employees covered under the scheme are entitled to medical facilities for self and dependants. They are also entitled to cash benefits in the event of specified contingencies resulting in loss of wages or earning capacity. The insured women are entitled to maternity benefit for confinement. Where death of an insured employee occurs due to employment injury or occupational disease, the dependants are entitled to family pension. Various benefits that the insured employees and their dependants are entitled to, the duration of benefits and contributory conditions thereof are as under:

Medical benefits

From day one of entering insurable employment for self and dependants such as spouse, parents and children own or adopted.

For self and spouse on superannuation subject to having completed five years in insurable employment on superannuation or in case of having suffered permanent physical disablement during the course of insurable employment.

Sickness benefits

oSickness benefit is payable to an insured person in cash, in the event of sickness resulting in absence from work and duly certified by an authorised insurable medical officer/ practitioner.

The benefit becomes admissible only after an insured has paid contribution for at least 78 days in a contribution period of 6 months.

Sickness benefit is payable for a maximum of 91 days in two consecutive contribution period.

Extended sickness benefit

Extended sickness benefit is payable to insured persons for the period of certified sickness in case of specified 34 long-term diseases that need prolonged treatment

and absence from work on medical advice.

For entitlement to this benefit an insured person should have been in insurable employment for at least 2 years. He/ she should also have paid contribution for a minimum of 156 days in the preceding 4 contribution periods or say 2 years.

ESI is payable for a maximum period of 2 years on the basis of proper medical certification and authentication by the designated authority.

Amount payable in cash as extended sickness benefit is payable within 7 days following the submission of complete claim papers at the local office concerned.

Enhanced sickness benefit

oThis cash benefit is payable to insured persons in the productive age group for under going sterilization operation, viz., vasectomy/ tubectomy. The contribution is the same as for the normal sickness benefit.

Enhanced sickness benefit is payable for 14 days for tubectomy and for seven days in case of vasectomy.

Maternity benefit

Maternity benefit is payable to insured women in case of confinement or miscarriage or sickness related thereto.

For claiming this an insured woman should have paid for at least 70 days in 2 consecutive contribution periods i.e. 1 year.

The benefit is normally payable for 12 weeks, which can be further extended up to 16 weeks on medical grounds.

The rate of payment of the benefit is equal to wage or double the standard sickness benefit rate.

oThe benefit is payable within 14 days of duly authenticated claim papers.

Disablement benefit

Disablement benefit is payable to insured employees suffering from physical disablement due to employment injury or occupation disease.

Dependants benefit

oDependants benefit [family pension] is payable to dependants of a deceased insured person where death occurs due to employment or occupational disease.

A widow can receive this benefit on a monthly basis for life or till remarriage. o A son or daughter can receive this benefit till 18 years of age.

Other dependants like parents including a widowed mother can also receive the benefit under certain condition.

The rate of payment is about 70% of the wages shareable among dependants in a fixed ratio.

The first installment is payable within a maximum of 3 months following the death of an insured person and thereafter, on a regular monthly basis.

Other benefits like funeral expenses, vocational rehabilitation, free supply of physical aids and appliances, preventive health care and medical bonus.

Obligations Of Employers

1.The employer should get his factory or establishments registered with the E.S.I. Corporation within 15 days after the Act becomes applicable to it, and obtain the employers Code Number.

2.The employer should obtain the declaration form from the employees covered under the Act and submit the same along with the return of declaration forms, to the E.S.I. office. He should arrange for the allotment of Insurance Numbers to the employees and their Identity Cards.

3.The employer should deposit the employees' and his own contributions to the E.S.I. Account in the prescribed manner, whether he has sufficient resources or not, his liability under the Act cannot be disputed. He cannot justify non-payment of E.S.I. contribution due to non- availability of finance.

4.The employer should furnish a Return of Contribution along with the challans of monthly payment, within 30 days of the end of each contribution period.

5.The employer should not reduce the wages of an employee on account of the contribution payable by him (employer).

6.The employer should cause to be maintained the prescribed records/registers namely the register of employees, the inspection book and the accident book.

7.The employer should report to the E.S.I. authorities of any accident in the place of employment, within 24 hours or immediately in case of serious or fatal accidents. He should make arrangements for first aid and transportation of the employee to the hospital. He should also furnish to the authorities such further information and particulars of an accident as may be required.

8.The employer should inform the local office and the nearest E.S.I. dispensary/hospital, in case of death of any employee, immediately.

9.The employer must not put to work any sick employee and allow him leave, if he has been issued the prescribed certificate.

10.The employer should not dismiss or discharge any employee during the period he/she is in receipt of sickness/maternity/temporary disablement benefit, or is under medical

Treatment, or is absent from work as a result of illness duly certified or due to pregnancy or confinement.

Records To Be Maintained For Inspection By ESI authorities

1.Attendance Register / Muster Roll
2.Salary / Wage Register / Payroll
3.EC (Employee's & Employer's Contribution) Statement
4.Employees' Register
5.Accident Book
6.Return of Contribution
7.Return of Declaration Forms
8.Receipted Copies of Challans

Employees Insurance Court

Any dispute arising under the ESI Act will be decided by the Employees Insurance Court and not by a Civil Court. It is constituted by the State Government for such local areas as may be specified and consists of such number of judges, as the Government may think fit. It shall adjudicate on the following disputes and claims.

Disputes as to:

i.Whether an employee is covered by the Act or whether he is liable to pay the contribution, or

ii.The rate of wages or average daily wages of an employee, or

iii.The rate of contribution payable by the employer in respect of any employee, or

iv.The person who is or was the principle employer in respect of any employee, or

v.The right to any benefit and the amount and duration thereof, or

vi.Any direction issued by the Corporation on a review of any payment of dependents benefit, or

vii.Any other matter in respect of any contribution or benefit or other due payable or recoverable under the Act.

Claims as to

i.Recovery of contributions from the principal employer,

ii.Recovery of contributions from a contractor,

iii.Recovery for short payment or non-payment of any contribution under section 68,

iv.Recovery of the value or amount of benefits received improperly under section 70,

v.Recovery of any benefit admissible under the Act

No dispute shall be admitted unless the employer deposits with the Court 50% of the amount due from him as claimed by the Corporation.

An appeal will lie to the High Court within 60 days against an order of the Employees Insurance Court if it involves a substantial question of law.

Important Forms to be submitted under the Act

EMPLOYEES PROVISIONS ACT, 1952 PROVIDENT FUND AND MISC.

An Act to provide for the institution of provident funds, pension funds and deposit linked insurance fund for the employees in the factories and other establishments. The Act extends to the whole of India except the State of Jammu and Kashmir.

Applicability

All factories and establishments in which 20 or more are employed

Schemes under the Act

Three beneficial schemes-

1. Employees Provident Fund Scheme 1952

2.Employees Pension Scheme 1995

3.Employees Deposit Linked Insurance 1976

Membership

An employee at the time of joining the employment and getting wages up to Rs.6500/- is required to become a member.

An employee is eligible for membership of fund from the very first date of joining a covered establishment.

Contribution to EPF

Employees' share : 12% of the Basic + DA

Employer's contribution : 12% to be deposited as :

8.33% to be deposited in Pension Fund A/C No 10 and

the balance, ie, 3.67% to be deposited in Provident Fund A/C No 01 along with

Employees' share of 12%

Administration charges -

@ 1.1% of the total wages/salary disbursed by deposit to A/C No 02,

Employees Deposit Linked Insurance @ 0.5% of the total wages/salary by deposit to A/C No. 21 and

Administration of EDLI @ 0.01% of the wages/ salary by deposit to A/C. No. 22.

Duties of employer

Employer to furnish information about:

(a)Ownership and names of responsible persons of the establishment.

(b)Declaration and nomination.

(c)Joining and leaving of service by the members in form 5 and form 10 respectively (d)Form 12A with monthly challans of deposit.

(e)Form 9 for details of employees.

(f)Form 3A/6A at the end of the financial year.

(g)Any other information as may be required under Para 76 of the scheme

Benefits to employees

 Provident Fund Benefits

Pension Benefits

Death Benefits

Provident Fund Benefits

Employer also contributes to Members' PF @ 3.67% (1.67% in case of sick industry - eg: beedi)

EPFO guarantees the Employer contribution and Govt. gives a decent interest to PF accumulations

Member can withdraw from this accumulations to cater financial exigencies in life - No need to refund unless misused

On resignation, the member can settle the account. i.e., the member gets his PF contribution, Employer Contribution and Interest

Pension Benefits

Pension to Member

Pension to Family (on death of member)

Scheme Certificate

o This Certificate shows the service & family details of a member

oThis is issued if the member has not attained the age of 58 while leaving an establishment and he applies for this certificate

oMember can surrender this certificate while joining another establishment and the service stated in the certificate is added with the service he is gaining from the new establishment.

oAfter attaining the age of 50 or above, the member can apply for Pension by surrendering this scheme certificate (if total service is at least 10 years)

This is a better choice than Withdrawal Benefit, that if a member dies holding a valid scheme certificate, his family will get pension (Death when NOT in service)

Withdrawal Benefit

- if not eligible for pension, member may withdraw the amount accumulated in his pension account
- the calculation of this amount is based only on (i) Last average salary and (ii) Service (Not based on actual amount available in Pension Fund Account)
- No amount is taken from Member to give Pension to the Member. Employer and Govt. contribute to Pension fund @8.33% and @1.16% respectively
- EPFO guarantees pension to members, even if the Employer has not contributed to Pension Fund.
- Pension calculation is similar to that of Govt. Employee
- Death Benefits
- Provident Fund Amount to Family (or to Nominee)
- Pension to Family (or to Parent / Nominee)

- Capital Return of Pension
- insurance (EDLI) amount to Family (or to Nominee)

•No amount is taken from Member for this facility. Employer contributes for this.
Nominee is basically determined as per the information submitted by the member at this office through FORM-2

Payment of Gratuity Act, 1972
Applicability of the Act
The Act provides for a scheme for the payment of gratuity to employees engaged in factories, mines, oilfields, plantations, ports, railway companies, shops or other establishments. The Act enforces the payment of 'gratuity', a reward for long service, as a statutory retiral benefit. Every employee irrespective of his wages is entitled to receive gratuity if he has rendered continuous service of 5 years or more than 5 years.

It is not paid to an employee gratuitously or merely as a matter of boon. It is paid for the service rendered by him to the employer (Delhi Cloth and General Mills Co; Ltd Vs the Workmen).
Gratuity is payable to an employee on termination of his employment after he has rendered continuous service for not less than five years:
on his superannuation
on his resignation
on his death or disablement due to employment injury or disease
The Working Journalists and Other Newspaper Employees (Conditions of service) and Miscellaneous Provisions Act, 1955, provides for payment of gratuity. As such, three years of continuous service is required for eligibility for Gratuity.

The payment of gratuity shall be forfeited:
to the extent of the damage or loss caused by the employee to the property of the employer
where the service of the employee is terminated due to misconduct
According to Sec.2(e) "employee" means any person (other than an apprentice) employed on wages, in any establishment, factory, mine, oilfield, plantation, port, railway company or shop, to do any skilled, semi-skilled, or unskilled, manual, supervisory, technical or clerical work, whether the terms of such employment are express or implied,[and whether or not such person is employed in a managerial or administrative capacity, but does not include any such person who holds a post under the Central Government or a State Government and is governed by any other Act or by any rules providing for payment of gratuity].

According to Sec.2A (1) an employee shall be said to be in continuous service for a period if he has, for that period, been in uninterrupted service, including service which may be interrupted on account of sickness, accident, leave, absence from duty without leave (not being absence in respect of which an order treating the absence as break in service has been passed in accordance with the standing order, rules or regulations governing the employees of the establishment), lay off, strike or a lock-out or cessation of work not due to any fault of the employee, whether such uninterrupted or interrupted service was rendered before or after the commencement of the Act. (2) where an employee (not being an employee employed in a seasonal establishment) is not in continuous service within the meaning of clause (1), for any period of one year or six months, he shall be deemed to be in continuous service under the employer

(a) for the said period of one year, if the employee during the period of twelve calendar months preceding the date with reference to which calculation is to be made, has actually worked under the employer for not less than -
(i)one hundred and ninety days, in the case of an employee employed below the ground in a mine or in an establishment which works for less than six days in a week; and
(ii)two hundred and forty days, in any other case;

      (c)   for the said period of six months, if the employee during the period of six calendar months preceding the date with reference to which the calculation is to be made, has actually worked under the employer for not less than –

(i)ninety-five days, in the case of an employee employed below the ground in a mine or in an establishment which works for less than six days in a week; and
(ii)one hundred and twenty days, in any other case;
Explanation: For the purpose of clause (2), the number of days on which an employee has actually worked under an employer shall include the days on which -
(i)he has been laid-off under an agreement or as permitted by standing orders made under the Industrial Employment (Standing Orders) Act, 1946 (20 of 1946), or under the Industrial Disputes Act, 1947 (14 of 1947), or under any other law applicab1c to the establishment;
(ii)he has been on leave with full wages, earned in the previous year;
(iii)he has been absent due to temporary disablement caused by accident arising out of and in the course of his employment and
(iv)in the case of a female, she has been on maternity leave; so, however, that the total period of such maternity leave does not exceed twelve weeks.

(3) where an employee employed in a seasonal establishment, is not in continuous service within the meaning of clause (1), for any period of one year or six months, he shall be deemed to be in continuous service under the employer for such period if he has actually worked for not less thanseventy-five per cent of the number of days on which the establishment was in operation during such period.

Rate of gratuity
For every completed year of service or part thereof in excess of six months, the employer shall pay gratuity to an employee at the rate of

fifteen days wages based on the rate of wages last drawn by the employee concerned.

In the case of a piece-rated employee, daily wages shall be computed on the average of the total wages received by him for a period of three months immediately preceding the termination of his employment, and, for this purpose, the wages paid for any overtime work shall not be taken into account.

In the case of an employee who is employed in a seasonal establishment and who is not so employed throughout the year, the employer shall pay the gratuity at the rate of seven days wages for each season.

In the case of a monthly rated employee, the fifteen days wages shall be calculated by dividing the monthly rate of wages last drawn by him by twenty-six and multiplying the quotient by fifteen.

The amount of gratuity payable to an employee shall not exceed three lakhs and fifty thousand rupees.

Responsibility of the Employer:

Every employer, other than an employer or an establishment belonging to, or under the control of, the Central Government or a State Government, shall, subject to the provisions of sub-section(2), obtain an insurance in the manner prescribed, for his liability for payment towards the gratuity under this Act, from the Life Insurance Corporation of India established under the Life Insurance Corporation of India Act, 1956 (31 of 1956) or any other prescribed insurer:

The appropriate Government may, subject to such conditions as may be prescribed, exempt every employer who had already established an approved gratuity fund in respect of his employees and who desires to continue such arrangement and every employer employing five hundred or more persons who establishes an approved gratuity fund in the manner prescribed.

Where an employer fails to make any payment by way of premium to the insurance or by way of 'contribution to all approved gratuity fund, he shall be liable to pay the amount of gratuity due

under this Act (including interest, if any, for delayed payments) forthwith to the controlling authority.

Whoever contravenes the provision above shall be punishable with fine which may extend to Rs 10,000/- and in the case of a continuing offence with a further fine which may extend to Rs 1000/- for each day during which the offence continues.

TAMILNADU PAYMENT OF SUBSISTENCE ALLOWENCE ACT 1981

Allowance given during action taken period (suspension, strike, legal action taken by organization) is called as subsistent allowance. It is enforced and enacted by the state government.

EMPLOYEE:

Employee is the person employed in the connection of the work or activity of any establishment to do any skill or semi-skill or unskilled or manual or supervisory or technical or reward or clerical for reward or hire but does not include person employed in managerial or in administration position.

EMPLOYER:
Employer is the owner of the establishment and includes any person entrusted with the supervision and control of the employees in such establishment.

ESTABLISHMENT:
Establishment is any place where any industry, trade, business, manufacturing, occupation/service is carried on but does not include railway administration, mining, oilfield and public sector.

SUSPENSION:
Suspension means a decision of any employer as a result which a employee temporarily from attend to his office and performing his function in the establishment on the   ground of enquiry into charge formed against the employee of pending or on final order is passed and implemented after the competition of enquiry.

PAYMENT OF SUBSISTENCE ALLOWENCE:
Any employee placed on supervision during supervision he entitled to receive the payment that payment is called as subsistent allowance:
Up to 90 days 50% of wage is given as the subsistence allowance
Up to 180 days 75% of wage is given as the subsistence allowance
After 180 days full wages is given as the subsistence allowance
If date is prolongs after 90 days which is attributable to the enquiry the allowance shall be reduced to 50% of wage
No subsistence allowance can received by an employee if he accept any other employment during the period of suspension
Subsistence allowance is paid by the employer to an employee on the due date but not on the day of the suspension.

RECOVERY OF MONEY DUE FROM EMPLOYEE:
If employee doesn't pay the subsistence allowance the employee or the authorized person or the legal representative in case of death can make an application to the government. The government will give him an opportunity to here. If satisfied it is directed to the collector who shall require the amount or pay from such employer. Such application (to recover money or allowance) can make within one year. An application shall be accepted after the expiry of one year if the government is satisfied on hearing the sufficient causes for not making application within one year.
PENALITY:
Fine or imprisonment for both employer and employee who violate the rules under this act.

TAMILNADU CONFIRMANT OF PERMENENTT STATUS ACT 1981:
This act is otherwise called as industrial establishment act

Applied to all factories, plantation, motor transport undertaking, shops and commercial establishment, catering establishment, and as notified by government.
Extended whole of Tamilnadu
Applicable to an established where the workmen are not less than 50 in number
It is applicable only after 2 years expiry of the establishment

DEFINITION:
EMPLOYER:
The person who has the ultimate control over the afire of the business or factory.

FACTORY:
In any premises where 10 or more persons are working in which a manufacturing process is carried on with the aid of power or 20 more workers are employed in which manufacturing process is carried on without the aid of power.

EMPLOYEE/LABOUR/WORKER:
Labor is defined as any person employed directly or through any agency weather with wage or not
CONFIRMANCE OF PERMENENT STATUS TO A WORKER:
Workmen who have continuous service of 480 in 24 months should be confirmed as permanent workers.

CONTINIOUS SERVICE:
UN interrupted services is required for the worker to become a permanent or to obtain permanent status. In case of any interruption:
- On account of sickness
- Accident
- Authorized league
- Legal strike
- Lockout
- Layoff
- Disablement (tempravory disablement)
- Stoppage of work not due to any fault on the employee
- In case of female employee maternity leave

INSPECTOR:
State government appoints the inspector for the purpose of act
Powers and duties of the inspector:
- Entering the premises with the assistant
- Verify weather act is implemented after the expire of 2 years since establishment
- Make examine of registers, records, notices, and take any spot evidence from any person working in the establishment
- Any information require by the inspector the employee should furnish all required information within 7 days

- • The act does not apply to the worker employed in the construction i.e. Building, dam, canal, bridges, roads, etc.

MAINTANENCE OF REGISTERER BY EMPLOYER:
1. FORM 1:
2. Serial no
3. Name and Address of employer
4. Destination
5. Weather tempravory, casual, substitute
6. Date of first entry to the service
7. Date or when the employee had completed 480 days of service
8. Date on which the employee made permanent
9. Remark and signature of the work men

THE WORKMEN'S COMPENSATION ACT, 1923
The Workmen's Compensation Act, aims to provide workmen and/or their dependents some relief in case of accidents arising out of and in the course of employment and causing either death or disablement of workmen.

It provides for payment by certain classes of employers to their workmen compensation for injury by accident.

Act does not apply where workman covered under ESI Act - Since a workman is entitled to get compensation from Employees State Insurance Corporation, a workman covered under ESI Act is not entitled to get compensation under Workmen's Compensation Act, as per section 53 of ESI Act, 1948.

Meaning of Workman (Sec.2 (n))
"Workman" means any person (other than a person whose employment is of a casual nature and who is employed otherwise than for the purposes of the employer's trade or business) who is - (i) a railway servant as defined in clause (34) of section 2 of the Railways Act, 1989 (24 of 1989), not permanently employed in any administrative, district or sub-divisional office of a railway and not employed in any such capacity as is specified in Schedule II, or (ia)

(a)a master, seaman or other member of the crew of a ship,

(b)a captain or other member of the crew of an aircraft,

(c)a person recruited as driver, helper, mechanic, cleaner or in any other capacity in connection with a motor vehicle,

(d) a person recruited for work abroad by a company, and who is employed outside India in any such capacity as is specified in Schedule II and the ship, aircraft or motor vehicle, or company, as the case may be, is registered in India, or

(ii) employed in any such capacity as is specified in Schedule II, whether the contract of employment was made before or after the passing of this Act and whether such contract is expressed or implied, oral or in writing; but does not include any person working in the capacity of a member of the Armed Forces of the Union; and any reference to a workman who has been injured shall, where the workman is dead, include a reference to his dependants or any of them.

The provisions of the Act have been extended to cooks employed in hotels, restaurants using power, liquefied petroleum gas or any other mechanical device in the process of cooking.

Employees Entitled To Compensation:

Every employee (including those employed through a contractor but excluding casual employees), who is engaged for the purposes of employers business and who suffers an injury in any accident arising out of and in the course of his employment, shall be entitled for compensation under the Act.

Employers Liability for Compensation (Accidents)

The employer of any establishment covered under this Act, is required to compensate an employee:

a.Who has suffered an accident arising out of and in the course of his employment, resulting into (i) death, (ii) permanent total disablement, (iii) permanent partial disablement, or (iv) temporary disablement whether total or partial, or

b.Who has contracted an occupational disease.

Employer Shall Not Be Liable:

a.In respect of any injury which does not result in the total or partial disablement of the workmen for a period exceeding three days;

b.In respect of any injury not resulting in death, caused by an accident which is directly attributable to-

i.the workmen having been at the time thereof under the influence or drugs, or

ii.the wilful disobedience of the workman to an order expressly given, or to a rule expressly framed, for the purpose of securing the safety of workmen, or

iii.the wilful removal or disregard by the workmen of any safeguard or other device which he knew to have been provided for the purpose of securing the safety of workmen.

The burden of proving intentional disobedience on the part of the employee shall lie upon the employer.

iv.when the employee has contacted a disease which is not directly attributable to a specific injury caused by the accident or to the occupation; or

v.when the employee has filed a suit for damages against the employer or any other person, in a Civil Court.

Contracting Out:

Any contract or agreement which makes the workman give up or reduce his right to compensation from the employer is null and void insofar as it aims at reducing or removing the liability of the employer to pay compensation under the Act.

Definition of Disablement

Disablement is the loss of the earning capacity resulting from injury caused to a workman by an accident.

Disablements can be classified as (a) Total, and (b) Partial. It can further be classified into (i) Permanent, and (ii) Temporary, Disablement, whether permanent or temporary is said to be total when it incapacitates a worker for all work he was capable of doing at the time of the accident resulting in such disablement.

Total disablement is considered to be permanent if a workman, as a result of an accident, suffers from the injury specified in Part I of Schedule I or suffers from such combination of injuries specified in Part II of Schedule I as would be the loss of earning capacity when totalled to one hundred per cent or more. Disablement is said to be permanent partial when it reduces for all times, the earning capacity of a workman in every employment, which he was capable of undertaking at the time of the accident. Every injury specified in Part II of Schedule I is deemed to result in permanent partial disablement.

Temporary disablement reduces the earning capacity of a workman in the employment in which he was engaged at the time of the accident.

Accident Arising Out Of And In The Course Of Employment
An accident arising out of employment implies a casual connection between the injury and the accident and the work done in the course of employment. Employment should be the distinctive and the proximate cause of the injury. The three tests for determining whether an accident arose out of employment are:

1.At the time of injury workman must have been engaged in the business of the employer and must not be doing something for his personal benefit;

2.That accident occurred at the place where he as performing his duties; and

3.Injury must have resulted from some risk incidental to the duties of the service, or inherent in the nature condition of employment.

Amount of compensation
The amount of compensation payable will be as follows, namely :-

(a)where death results an amount equal to fifty per cent of the monthly wages of the deceased workman multiplied by the relevant factor; or an amount of fifty thousand rupees, whichever is more;

(b)where permanent total an amount equal to disablement results from sixty the injury per cent of the monthly wages of the injured workman multiplied by the relevant factor, or an amount of sixty thousand rupees, whichever is more; For the purposes of clause (a) and clause (b), "relevant factor", in relation to a workman means the factor specified in the second column of Schedule IV against the entry in the first column of that Schedule specifying the number of years which are the same as the completed years of the age of the workman on his last birthday immediately preceding the date on which the compensation fell due. Where the monthly wages of a workman exceed two thousand rupees, his monthly wages for the purposes of clause (a) and clause (b) shall be deemed to be two thousand rupees only;

(c)where permanent partial disablement results from the injury (i) in the case of an injury specified in Part II of Schedule I, such percentage of the compensation which would have been payable in the

case of permanent total disablement as is specified therein as being the percentage of the loss of earning capacity caused by that injury, and (ii) in the case of an injury not specified in Schedule I, such percentage of the compensation payable in the case of permanent total disablement as is proportionate to the loss of earning capacity (as assessed by the qualified medical practitioner) permanently caused by the injury;

(d) Where temporary a half monthly payment of the sum disablement, whether equivalent totwenty-five per cent of total or partial, results monthly wages of the workman, to from the injury be paid in accordance with the provisions of sub-section (2).

(1A) Notwithstanding anything contained in sub-section (1), while fixing the amount of compensation payable to a workman in respect of an accident occurred outside India, the Commissioner shall take into account the amount of compensation, if any, awarded to such workman in accordance with the law of the country in which the accident occurred and shall reduce the amount fixed by him by the amount of compensation awarded to the workman in accordance with the law of that country.

(2) The half-monthly payment referred to in clause (d) of sub-section (1) shall be payable on the sixteenth day - (i) from the date of disablement where such disablement lasts for a period of twenty- eight days or more; or

(ii) after the expiry of a waiting period of three days from the date of disablement where such disablement lasts for a period of less than twenty-eight days; and thereafter half-monthly during the disablement or during a period of five years, whichever period is shorter : Provided that - (a) there shall be deducted from any lump sum or half-monthly payments to which the workman is entitled the amount of any payment or allowance which the workman has received from the employer by way of compensation during the period of disablement prior to the receipt of such lump sum or of the first half-monthly payment, as the case may be; and (b) no half-monthly payment shall in any case exceed the amount, if any, by which half the amount of the monthly wages of the workman before the accident exceeds half the amount of such wages which he is earning after the accident. Explanation : Any payment or allowance which the workman has received from the employer towards his medical treatment shall not be deemed to be a payment or allowance received by him by way of compensation within the meaning of clause (a) of the proviso.

(3)On the ceasing of the disablement before the date on which any half-monthly payment falls due, there shall be payable in respect of that half-month a sum proportionate to the duration of the disablement in that half-month.

(4)If the injury of the workman results in his death, the employer shall, in addition to the compensation under sub-section (1), deposit with the Commissioner a sum of one thousand rupees for payment of the same to the eldest surviving dependant of the workman towards the expenditure of the funeral of such workman or where the workman did not have a dependant or was not living with his dependant at the time of his death to the person who actually incurred such expenditure

General principles of the Act

There must be a casual connection between the injury and the accident and the work done in the course of employment;

The onus is upon the applicant to show that it was the work and the resulting strain which contributed to or aggravated the injury;

It is not necessary that the workman must be actually working at the time of his death or that death must occur while he was working or had just ceased to work; and

Where the evidence is balanced, if the evidence shows a greater probability which satisfies a reasonable man that the work contributed to the causing of the personal injury it would be enough for the workman to succeed. But where the accident involved a risk common to all humanity and did not involve any peculiar or exceptional danger resulting from the nature of the employment or where the accident was the result of an added peril to which the workman by his own conduct exposed himself, which peril was not involved in the normal performance of the duties of his employment, then the employer will not be liable.

Employer's fault is immaterial

The compensation is payable even when there was no fault of employer. In New India Assurance Co. Ltd. v. Pennamna Kuriern - (1995) 84 Comp. Cas. 251 (Ker HC DB), claim of workmen for compensation under Motor Vehicle Act was rejected due to negligence of employee, but compensation was awarded under Workmen's Compensation Act on the principle of 'no fault'.

Compensation payable even if workman was careless

Compensation is payable even if it is found that the employee did not take proper precautions. An employee is not entitled to get compensation only if (a) he was drunk or had taken drugs (b) he wilfully disobeyed orders in respect of safety (c) he wilfully removed safety guards of machines. However, compensation cannot be denied on the ground that workman was negligent or careless. –

Mar Themotheous v. Santosh Raj 2001 LLR 164 (Ker HC DB).

Number of Workmen Employed Is Not Criteria

In definition of 'workman' in schedule II, in most of the cases, number of workmen employed is not the criteria. In most of cases, employer will be liable even if just one workman is employed. The Act applies to a workshop even if it employs less than 20 workmen and is not a 'factory' under Factories

Act. – Sunil Industries v. Ram Chander 2000 AIR SCW 4109 = 2001 LLR 64 = 2000(7) SCALE 415.

Payment of compensation only through Commissioner - A Commissioner for Workmen's

Compensation is appointed by Government. The compensation must be paid only through the Commissioner in case of death or total disablement. Any lump sum payment to workman under the Act must be made only through Commissioner. Direct payment to workman or his dependents is not recognized at all as compensation

CONTACT	
CREATOR	T.M.SURESH
ABOUT PROJECT MSW	CONVERSION OF SOCIAL WORK STUDY MATERIALS (IN PAPER) INTO SOFT COPIES, ELIMINATING THE DIFFUCILTIES IN GETTING STUDY MATERIALS.